MEMORIES OF NORWICH

IN OUR OWN WORDS

A Collection of Memories
from The People of Norwich

Edited by
Sarah Housden

Published by
Norwich Living History Group

© 2010 Norwich Living History Group

28 Racecourse Road
Norwich
NR7 9HX
www.reminiscence4life.co.uk

ISBN 978-0-9563255-2-5

Published by Norwich Living History Group
Illustrations by Linda McAllister www.reminiscence-resources.com

Cover design and typesetting by
Chandler Book Design, Kings Lynn, UK

Printing and binding by
MPG Biddles, Kings Lynn, UK

Published by

NORWICH LIVING HISTORY GROUP

CONTENTS

ACKNOWLEDGEMENTS

Apart from our gratitude to the thirteen prospective writers who have contributed their memories of Norwich to this book, Norwich Living History Group also wishes to thank Margaret Plummer, Sue Steward, Jenny Zmroczek and Linda McAllister for the time they took to read through each of the entries to the autobiographical writing competition, and for the honest appraisals they gave in response to each entry.

In addition, we wish to thank the Picture Norfolk website (http://norlink.norfolk.gov.uk), run by Norfolk County Council for giving permission to base the illustration of Read's Flour Mill on a Bridewell Museum (NCC) image (Bridewell ref: 4.516.21).

INTRODUCTION

In August 2009, Norwich Living History Group launched an autobiographical writing competition, inviting the people of Norwich to submit entries based on their memories of living and working in the city. *Memories of Norwich: In our own words* is a collection of writing based on those entries.

Within this volume you will find a wide variety of writing, in different styles and reflecting memories from a range of eras, which we put forward primarily because we feel the images portrayed in these stories have great potential to stimulate the memories of readers, and hence to generate further autobiographical writing, discussion and reminiscence, and perhaps too, to provide the incentive for readers who have not yet done so, to record their own memories with Norwich Living History Group. Our aim is that future generations might benefit from the wealth of knowledge and experience that exists in the memories of local people.

Such memories, we consider, are also of worth as a source of material for scholars of social history, in both the present and future, who seek to gain a fuller picture of what life was like for ordinary people in Norwich in the twentieth century. Within this book there is a wealth of information concerning local shops, businesses, cinemas and schools, interspersed with stories which tell us about the attitudes of society, the trials, adventures and ambitions of youth, and the general living and working conditions of past decades.

It is likely that the reader will find some styles and topics of writing more to their liking than others. Indeed, this collection represents a diverse range of perspectives, with some writers taking a comic stance in the telling of their stories, while others have a note of sadness - a natural reflection of the material shared.

Norwich Living History Group is a non profit making organisation, run by volunteers, which aims to promote interest in and enjoyment of the history of Norwich in the twentieth century. Any profits from the sale of this book will be used to continue our work. Readers inspired to put pen to paper themselves, or who wish to make an oral recording of their memories, are welcome to contact the Editor by writing to the publisher's address or via our website (www.reminiscence4life.co.uk).

Finally, we hope you enjoy reading this collection and our thanks and congratulations go to everyone whose writing is included in *Memories of Norwich: In our own words.*

Sarah Housden
Chair of Norwich Living History Group

Saturday – Before the War

Roy William Foyster, born 1929

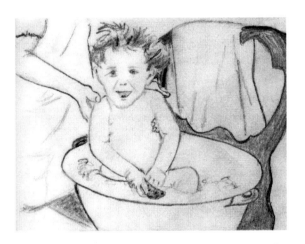

Yawn! Oh it's morning. What day is it? What did I do yesterday? Oh yes, I had a bath, so it must have been Friday, when the galvanised bath is brought into the kitchen from the shed and the kitchen copper is filled and lit, burning old wooden shoe lasts from the shoe factory that Dad works at.

The whole family has baths on Friday night and washes their hair, "Friday night is Amami night" as the advert for shampoo says.

The best part is emptying the bath, the water can be ladled into the sink but the bath has handles at each end and Mum and Dad heave it into the back yard and tip the water over the concrete to wash that as well.

Well, its Saturday, no school, so what is there to do? What's that? A steady scuffling and lots of shouting. Let's look out of the window - oh yes, it's the cattle on the way to market, being driven in from the country by men helped by gig boys who go 'bullock whopping' for a penny or two. These bullocks are on their way to the Cattle Market behind the Castle. The cattle drives cause all sorts of problems when a bullock darts up the passageway between houses and gets into the backyards where it is very difficult to turn them round and get them back on the road. Children and women run into shops and front gardens and shut the gates to escape them, and it has been said that the cattle get into shops too. They also leave an awful lot of mess on the road!

Oh, here is another sight and sound; the clip-clop of hooves and rumble of wheels as the brewery horses of Steward and Patteson haul their carts and drays piled high with cases and barrels of beer on the way to deliver to public houses in the city and country. The city carts are smaller with rubber tyres and pulled by one horse, but the country ones are huge with iron-shod wheels and pulled by two or even four very big shire horses to visit many pubs outside the city.

The men are very big as well, for they have to heave giant barrels of beer off the cart and into the cellars of the pubs.

When the carts return late in the day, loaded with empty barrels, the men are often asleep after drinking many pints of beer at all the pubs they visit, but the horses know their own way home and plod steadily on to the brewery in Barrack Street. The stables are on an upper floor and you can see the horses looking out.

The brewery also has a steam boat called 'Annie' which is kept down 'The Cut' in Barrack Street. This boat takes beer by river to Great Yarmouth. My next door neighbour, Mr Frank Royal, is the skipper of this boat and sometimes he takes me to see it. It is painted bright blue, and so are all the doors in his house!

Well what else is there to do on a Saturday morning? I could go to the pictures if I had some money, either to the 'penny pictures' in the hall behind the Co-op in Magdalen Street, but they are all old silent films; or over the street to the 'tuppenny rush' in the 'Cinema' - but that's so rough and noisy with the kids in the fourpenny seats upstairs throwing orange-peel onto those below. Maybe I'll go to the new 'Odeon' in Botolph Street where the 'Mickey Mouse Club' is held and everyone sings:

"Every Saturday morning.

Where do we go?

Getting into mischief?

Oh dear no

To the Mickey-Mouse club

With our badges on

Every Saturday morning

At the O-DE-ON"

But even some of the well-behaved Mickey Mousers will go to the lavatory and open the exit doors from the inside to let in some pals who have no money to get in.

I believe you can get into the 'Empire' cinema with a jam jar, but I've never been there because they say it's a flea-pit

Oh! What is happening now? It's the lorry delivering fish to the fish and chip shop over the road. The fish is all packed in ice and comes from Lowestoft each day. Maybe I can go over later to see them gutting and filleting the fish - it all comes as it was caught and has to be prepared in the shed behind the shop. The potatoes come in sacks and have to be cleaned before they are peeled in a big container that turns, with water pouring through it. All the potatoes are made into chips using a hand chopper, as they are needed in the shop.

The man at the fish shop has to light the fire under the pans each day. The fire has to be fed with coal all the while the shop is open. It's a good fish and chip shop and you can get a ha'pworth of chips with some batter crisps wrapped in newspaper; they're delicious.

If I get my Saturday penny I may go to Miss Chapman's shop on the corner of Spencer Street and Silver Street for some sweets, perhaps a liquorice telephone or liquorice shoelaces for a farthing or some tiger nuts or liquorice root or jap nuggets or a lucky bag or a sherbet dip, or even have a go on the punch board where, if you are lucky, you might punch out a paper to win a bar of chocolate; or if you are unlucky – nothing.

Miss Chapman's shop is a wonderful place selling everything from paraffin which is pumped from a big tank in the shop, to groceries, vegetables and even medicines which she measures and pours into a glass which you take to the shop. She has Syrup of Figs for the children and Syrup of Bucktham for Spot, our dog, who hates it - but so do I hate Syrup of Figs.

Maybe Mum will want me to go 'down the street' (Magdalen Street) for some shopping; perhaps she will want some new 'art-silk' stockings from Aunty Lily's wool shop at Magdalen Gates, or a new Van Heusen shirt collar for Dad from the men's shop further down near the new Belisha Beacon crossing near the Blind School. If I have to go to the Co-op I must remember Aunt Hilda's dividend number: its eleven, six, five, nine. She will get money back later for everything she buys. Maybe I'll go to the 'Home and Colonial' shop for groceries or to Sturten's for some soda or a Reckitts 'blue-bag' for rinsing the washing. Then I can look in "Little Woolies" (Woolworths), where everything costs either threepence or sixpence, or across the street to Bremner's Bazaar where the floor slopes and everything is even cheaper.

On the way back I can go into Halfords to look at the Dinky Toy cars and Hornby trains; maybe I will meet my friend Alan who has a lot of pocket money and buys a Dinky Toy one Saturday and a Hornby truck the next – perhaps I will go up to his to play with his trains and cars in his garden.

What else can I do? Maybe I will go to see Mr Howard who lives about six doors away and has a green and white painted workshop where he repairs shoes and makes all sorts of things – he has a funny saying if anything is special – he says: "That's a Rumsky Skumsby funny one".

If I'm lucky he may take me to the cattle market and we will follow the cattle trail along Bull Close Road, down Bull Close, along Cowgate and across Tombland to the market by the Castle. There are hundreds of bullocks and cows at the front of the market, with sheep near the Castle and pigs opposite; all in pens and all making a lot of noise, smell and mess.

At the top of the market is a covered area where you can see chickens, ducks, geese, rabbits, puppies and kittens, all in cages and for sale. Even better, round the corner is the horse sales ring where lovely horses and ponies are on show.

Sometimes there is a shout saying an animal is loose and everyone runs around trying to catch the bullock or pig, or even sometimes a bull that has escaped. It's great fun, but a bit frightening.

At the front of the Cattle Market is the Agricultural Hall where they sell all sorts of farm tools and supplies. Sometimes they have big exhibitions there and once I got a huge pencil, about an inch thick, with Bourne-Vita printed on it: I believe it's a bedtime drink. I like going with Mr Howard to the cattle market.

Is it time to have a haircut yet? If it is I can go to Billy Barney's shop over the road and have a 'short-back-and-sides' for threepence; men's' haircuts are sixpence and they also have shaves. It looks very dangerous when Mr Barney lathers their chins and then cuts the whiskers off with a long knife called a 'cut-throat razor'. It is very sharp because Mr Barney sharpens it on a strap before he starts shaving. They say that barbers learn to shave by practising on balloons - if it bursts they have to start again. After the shave the men have a hot flannel on their faces. Barney's is better than Dady's in Cowgate where men go to have a 'fourpenny all off'.

Well that should take me up to dinnertime when Dad comes home from work at the shoe factory; we will probably have fish and chips today.

Now how about this afternoon? I suppose Mum might take me and my new sister up the city to the new market place near the new City Hall. It's alright I suppose, but it's not so interesting as the old market where all sorts of stalls were spread over the area selling lots of fruit, vegetables, meat, fish, flowers, sweets and at the 'back of the market', all sorts of goods like pots and pans, plates and dishes, clothes and anything you needed. The stalls had 'naptha' lamps, which hissed and smelled and gave a very white light. Now it's all tidy with new stalls which are cleaned away into a store on Saturday night, and the whole area is cleaned. On Sunday it is used for meetings and the Salvation Army Band plays; people on boxes shout at the people about all sorts of things.

Perhaps we will go into "Big Woolies", near the market, which stays open till about eight o'clock when the market people are selling all the fruit, vegetables and meat cheaply and lots of people come to get a bargain.

If we didn't have the pram to walk home we could catch the bus from Orford Place to Magdalen Gates, it costs a penny for grown-ups and a halfpenny for children. It's not as good as the trams used to be when you could go on top and there was not a roof - the seats had backs that flapped backwards and forwards so you could face either way. The tram picked up electricity from wires over the street by a long arm with a pulley on it which ran along the wire; it used to spark when it ran over joins in the wire. When the tram went round the corner near the main post office the wheels would groan and screech against the rails. No, buses aren't such fun.

I hope Norwich City are playing at home 'cause Dad might take me there instead of going to the city. It's a long walk to the new football ground at Carrow Road. We go down Bull Close Road past the Boys' Brigade Hall and along Barrack Street where the new blocks of flats have been built, and past the Barracks where all the soldiers live. There is a lane that goes down by the river near the Cow Tower; the river is very dirty with all sorts of nasty stuff from factories, breweries, the Gas works and the Tannery factory which all have drains into the river. Fish which are caught here have blue spots all over them, but children still swim in the river. Along Riverside Road you can see the river and the Sea Cadets ship, the Lord Nelson, with a big mast and rigging which the boys climb.

We may see lighters, which are like barges, full of coal being taken up river to the Gas Works. The lightermen work the boats along by starting at the front and pushing a long pole, called a quant, into the river bed and they lean on the end of the pole and walk along the edge of the lighter; but although they walk they stay still and it's the boat that moves forward. When the man gets to the back of the boat he lifts his quant out of the water and carries it to the front and starts all over again: it looks very hard work.

Near the railway station we will see lots of 'fly-sheets' for Sunday newspapers saying they will be reporting today's match tomorrow.

Further along riverside will be big steamships unloading coal, timber, steel, grain and all sorts of goods up river from the sea at Great Yarmouth. There is a bridge at Carrow Road that lifts up to let these big ships through, but they don't open it on match days when people have to cross the river to get to the football ground.

It's a bit frightening to have to wait at the boys' turnstile and then have to find Dad inside, but it's usually alright. We always go round the pitch to stand on the halfway line on the terrace, which is made of thousands of old railway sleepers laid on a sloping bank. Opposite us is a building called The Stand, but it is where people sit - I can't understand that.

Dad buys a bar of 'Caley's Marching Chocolate' for our half time treat, from a boy with a tray full of sweets. The chocolate is very dark and very hard and so sweet it is almost bitter. It is made in Norwich near Chapelfield Gardens. They say it was made to give soldiers energy on the march.

The football is always exciting and I wonder how the players can head the heavy leather ball without getting hurt, especially when it's wet. I once got hit in the face by a football when Dad was playing one Sunday morning in a kick-about on a pitch in the Valley Drive on Mousehold Heath – it hurt a lot. I was only four years old then.

After the match we walk all the way home and sometimes call into Kahlers the bakers shop in Cowgate and buy some pastries for tea. They sell them at seven for sixpence because it's late on Saturday and they can't keep them. We get cream horns, apple puffs, Banbury's vanilla slices, conserves, madeleines - all delicious, and carry them home up Bull Close.

The most important event of the day comes next when Dad says, "Quiet please" and takes down the football results from the wireless to see if we have won the pools – we never do. After tea I will have to go across the road to the paper shop to get the *Pink Un* so that Dad can read all about the match he went to see and check the football results all over again.

We listen to 'In-town-tonight' on the wireless, where there is lots of traffic noise and a man shouts "Stop!" and it all goes quiet and then he says: "Once again we stop the mighty roar of London's traffic to bring you some of the interesting people who are 'In town tonight.'" Afterwards it will be time for me to go to bed.

I may watch people in the fish shop for a while and when it's dark watch the reflections of bicycle lights going across the ceiling. If I am awake at ten o'clock I'll listen to the people coming out of the Bull public house next door and calling "Goodnight Eadie", "Goodnight Fred", "Goodnight George". Why don't they say goodnight in the pub becore they come out?

Ah well, that's Saturday sorted out. Now I had better get up and start it all!

Schooldays

Grace Dearn, born 1926

In August 1919 Ernest and Elsie Dearn were married at St George Tombland, both being 23 years old. Throughout the war, Ernest served in the RAMC and Elsie worked at Harmers Clothing Factory, making army uniforms. They were my parents. Seven years later, I was born. We lived in a cottage in Cook's Court, Pottergate.

At four years old I went to Willow Lane School. This lasted for one and a half days, as a bigger girl upset me, and Mum took me home. My sister came along then. We were allocated a council house in Cadge Road to accommodate our growing family. This road consisted of forty houses in 1930, and we knew all the residents. At five years old, school was compulsory – I was soon integrated into Wensum View 'Mixed Infants' Department. A bus transported us to and from school. I was scared of everyone – teachers, bigger children, and boys – anyone in authority.

Dad worked for British Gas Light Co on repairs, and later as a meter collector. Mum did not work, so I would expect her to be there when school was over. Most Mums did not go out to work in those days.

Free milk was supplied at school. We were allowed to take lunch – a small sandwich, or similar – our names written on the pack, which was placed in a box at the classroom doorway. As food was always important to me, it caused me great distress if anyone ever took my lunch.

Mum attended my medical examination at school, which was fine. We then went back to my classroom. I rushed in, leaving Mum at the door – not even a 'Goodbye', so anxious was I to get back. I was not so keen to do the lesson, but thought I would be in trouble if I was away too long.

At regular times we would be weighed and measured. Also, a nurse (who we called the 'flea nurse') came to look at our hair. I do not remember anyone being sent home with nits or fleas, but I expect there must have been. Diphtheria and scarlet fever were dreaded illnesses, necessitating hospital admission. The Fever Ambulance was a cause for concern; children were very afraid of catching 'something bad'.

My first report said "She is backward with her reading". As soon as possible, Mum took me to the library and I soon learnt to enjoy reading. We all had our own desk in class, with the blackboard and teacher at the front. Times tables and spellings were chanted before lessons every day.

Fortunately Dad was in regular work, earning £2 10s 0d a week. It had to be used carefully to pay for everything.

In the holidays we would take a picnic, mainly to Earlham Park very nearby, and occasionally, if there was enough money, Mum would take us to the City by bus. A walk through Cathedral Close and up St James' Hill, on to Mousehold Heath was a great treat. I knew nobody who owned a car in those days.

I have indicated that I was afraid of everybody, including boys, but Mum had a friend who visited us who had a son George, and he was not a threat. At the end of one school term a party was arranged. Girls were invited to take their favourite doll – the boys would judge and give the winner a rosette. I thought my doll looked beautiful – how could George resist her? But sadly he did. I did not like him so much after that.

On May 24th an important event took place. We dressed in best clothes, took our Union Flags, and were taught a display – usually dancing or singing. The Lord Mayor would come to watch, awarding us a half day's holiday.

In 1936 we moved to a bigger house in George Borrow Road, and to Dad's delight, there was a bigger garden – his favourite hobby next to his association with the British Red Cross was gardening. As a family, we were all active at St Anne's Church.

Colman Road School was now in our catchment area, and I was in the last year of Junior School. The conversation at this time was always the prospect of war – I believe the boys enjoyed frightening us with all their tales of what might happen.

Lessons did not come easily to me. I would have loved to have passed to enter Grammar School, but although I passed the first part, and the interview, that was all. I was now in the Senior School at Colman Road. It was quite pleasant there and I settled down to stay until I was fourteen – the school leaving age. We learned to sew and knit, as well as cooking, alongside the usual subjects. In May 1937 the Norwich City Council presented us with a book called 'Kingship' to commemorate the coronation of King George VI, and Queen Elizabeth. I still have my copy.

In 1938 I was chosen, along with other young people my age from various local schools, to be present at the official opening of Norwich City Hall. We sat on benches each side of the main entrance to watch the King and Queen carry out the ceremony. Afterwards the Market Traders gave us a bag of fruit and sweets. Later in the day we went to Dereham Road, near Lakenham Lane, to wave to the departing Royalty.

About this time I heard it was possible to take an examination for admission to the Norwich City College, Junior Commercial School. I had set my mind on an office job, and this seemed most desirable. There were only about seventy places each year, so I did not count my chances too highly, but I went for it.

The 'war news' got worse. It now seemed certain war was coming soon. Preparations were in hand for shelters, blackouts, gas masks and identity cards. Some parents sent their children to Canada and other places overseas to keep them away from air raids. Other children were evacuated to country areas.

On Sunday 3rd September 1939 the news broke that Great Britain was at war with Germany. It was broadcast by radio. As we were at church at the time, Dad, who was the Churchwarden, had to go home to listen to the news. He came back and signed to the Vicar, who made the announcement (there were no mobile phones or portable radios in those days!) The siren sounded the same day – I am sure we all thought the invasion had happened – but the all-clear sounded soon afterwards. We would hear it many more times in the future.

About this time I heard my application and examination to the Commercial School had been successful. I was pleased, but the war over-shadowed it. Not only was there the fear of enemy action, but also questions about where we would be educated. Our school had been taken over as a Decontamination Centre in case of gas attacks, but after a short delay we were accommodated at Blackfriars Hall, which was divided by curtains into four classrooms. Despite this, it was quiet and well organised.

The siren frequently interrupted our lessons. We would be instructed to take our gas masks and proceed to the cloisters of St Andrew's Hall. There, our gas masks were checked by a member of staff – a blotting pad was placed on the snout of the respirator and we had to breathe in. This would hold the pad in place. If it did not, adjustments were made to the straps, until it worked. I hated this, and prayed we would never have to use them for real. My prayer was answered.

After a few months at Blackfriars Hall the headmaster at Nelson School, Mr Nursey, made arrangements for us to take over some of the classrooms there. This was much better and easier for us all. Our lessons were still disrupted by air raid sirens and we spent hours in the underground shelters in the playground. Miss Clunie, the shorthand teacher, would even teach us outlines in the shelter. We would also play games like Lexicon. There never seemed to be enemy planes about, but we discovered afterwards that a lot was going on in the south of England. What would become known as 'The Battle of Britain' was taking place. If we were still in the shelters when it was time to go home, we had to wait there until a parent arrived. My Dad often came to meet me, taking me home on the seat of his bicycle.

It was a wonder we ever learned anything! I was still finding the work difficult, but I persevered and finally grasped the shorthand outlines. Some of the other subjects were also beginning to make sense. Touch-typing needed to be mastered, and I will always remember the day my fingers began to find the keys without having to look. Miss Wells, who taught this subject, always encouraged us. "You will not look back now", she said. There was still some way to go but it gradually became second nature. I did manage a 60 words per minute shorthand examination and a Pitman and RSA typing examination, before leaving the school at fifteen.

I will not claim to be the greatest shorthand writer or typist who ever lived, but I owe my working life (which was 50 years) to the Commercial School, which opened up many interesting jobs and life experiences for me. But that's another story...

THE BOTHWOPS

Anna Bentley, born 1963

The Bentleys lived in NR4, on Mile End Road. There were four of us (big sister, me, little sister and little brother) and our parents, Sid and Doris. Newmarket Road was our stomping ground. We all went to Colman Middle School, then Bowthorpe. I should really have gone to CNS or the Hewitt: that's where all my friends went. So where did I go? Bowthorpe! Why, you may ask, would I go there? It was such a long walk. Well, there was a very good reason. My older sister went there, so whatever we put on the form as my first choice of school, I would get Bowthorpe anyway, so we put it first.

And it was a long walk : past Colman Primary; over 'Cap'n Bird's Eye's' lollipop crossing; past the first lot of shops with the sweet shop that sold Flying Saucers, Milk Teeth, Love Hearts, Shoe Laces...; the second lot of shops with the shoe shop (and the high-heeled sandals I wanted and finally got), the cake shop, the chemist, the pub my friend's parents owned and the library where I took out Lady Chatterley's Lover as soon as I could go into the grown-up section; then houses, a long road, a roundabout, and past the cemetary. Turn left into Bowthorpe Road and it was on the right. Bowthorpe School.

Before Bowthorpe Comprehensive was born it was Henderson junior mixed, opened in 1942. In 1948 this became Gurney Girls and Henderson Boys, and in 1968 it re-merged into Gurney Henderson Co-Ed Secondary School. Those names lived on in the girls' and boys' gyms, the assembly halls and the two wings of classrooms when, in 1970, it was finally renamed Bowthorpe Comprehensive. I even met somebody in Norwich who went to Henderson in his younger days. I wonder if the boys had to do then what they did when I was there: I would sit in Mr Fuller's maths class, upstairs at the front corner of Henderson wing, watching poor little boys dragging themselves round the perimeter of the football pitch, over and over again.

I wonder how many of them met 'Charlie', Killer Kilshaw's plimsol? I met somebody I did not know at school, whose backside had been in contact with 'Charlie'. Mr Kilshaw, now a neighbour of mine, tells me the production of 'Charlie' was a rather solemn event.

One of my oldest friends was a fellow sixth-former at Bowthorpe. (She went to Costessey High, but they had no sixth form so we had an annual invasion.) We acted together in school plays and musicals – something the Drama teacher put on every year. We worked with him after we left school as well, performing 'Trudi and the Minstrel' with a theatre company in Norwich, this time with adults. The link with Costessey was marked in the 1981 magazine, with a brilliantly illustrated article in which 'Costley meets Bothwop'.

I have copies of the Magazine from 1976 to 1981, all the years I was there. They are full of poems and stories, all illustrated with lino prints and drawings. There are photographs of trips to Blakeney Point, the Yorkshire Moors and further flung places, such as Russia, where my younger sister went. I got a really nice job in later years partly because I could read Cyrillic! Does anyone remember Mr Manoff's jumper? There is an article about work experience in a hospital, written by my older sister, saying that she wants to be a nurse when she is older. Now she is a Community Nurse and a Sister, and has at least ten years' experience on a surgical ward. Bowthorpe must have done something right.

So, imagine my shock when, during a driving lesson, when I was about 29 years old, my instructor directed me to turn into Bowthorpe Road, to pull up on the left and look to my right. There was my old school, razed to the ground.

I suppose it was no longer 'viable', but I think it had a good ethos, and a great team of staff, who remain good friends, and who continue to support their former pupils. Looking back, I can see that it had been allowed to run down before closure. The toilets were never fragrant or sparkling, with thick paint and hard, shiny paper, migrating seats and cold water! A favourite memory is a summoning of all the girls in the school to the Henderson Hall for a 'special' assembly with the Deputy Head, Miss Brighty. She got so angry about the girls who were throwing unspeakable items around the toilets that she got the first letter of 'mucking about' wrong, resulting in thunderous shaking of shoulders throughout the assembled company.

It was very sad to see the end of the place where I spent six of the most productive years of my life. All the girls had to do metalwork and woodwork, and the boys needlework and cookery, and vice versa of course. I still have the smocking sampler that I finished while sitting on the grass bank during the school sports day one year. History consisted of wattle and daub houses and the feudal system. I did not do A Level geography, but I started it, and we had one textbook to share, making homework challenging. I am quite familiar with the life cycle of the frog and the dissection of worms.

Parent Teacher Association evenings were brightened up with performances by 'Troubador', the vocal quintet started by the guitar-playing Drama teacher, who took us to sing in 'Old Folks Homes' around Norwich. The Music teacher organised really memorable trips for the two of us who did A Level, including a visit to Ursula Vaughan Williams, one to Lennox Berkeley, a visit to Willy Bailey's instrument-making studio, and a recording of one of the teacher's compositions with Stuart Orr, who interviewed us about the teacher's invented musical instrument, the 'Crungeaphone' on Radio Norfolk. A clue to that teacher's identity is that one could be 'Crandellised'!

A few weeks ago I drove into the old Bowthorpe School site with my 13 year old niece, so that she could see where her Mum (my 'little' sister) went to school. The front fence is still there, but the grass is now scrubby and overgrown. There are new houses off the driveway, where the dinner hut and exam hut used to be. Further up you can see the mark of the foundations where the gyms were – the sixth form boys who had 'fizzies' - that's mopeds - and even cars would park between them, near the entrance, like the teachers. There is now a fire station where the art and science rooms were, and the playground at the furthest end is now a car park, but the view across what used to be the running track and sports field is still there.

My niece asked lots of questions, which helped me remember the sixth form room above the music block. For the less academic there was a greenhouse; for broody girls there was 'the flat' where they could cook meals for their parents and teachers. For practical boys there was always an old car in the mechanics room as well as TD (Technical Drawing). Aspiring typists sat in rows keeping time to Radio 1 upstairs in Gurney Wing, and for the rarefied few nerds, there was an enormous computer in a small room near Henderson Hall.

Bowthorpe School was a good school for me, but now it's gone, except in the minds of those who remember it. Earlham is the local school now, recently promoted to Academy status. They were our arch rivals then, though I'm sure we must have gone to the same chip shop. That's still there too – and it's still the best.

A Never Forgotten Experience

Valerie Turner

It was as I was stirring minced beef on the cooker hob that the childhood memory came flooding back; a memory of how my clever, young mother, who had been called back into war work while her sister Flora looked after me and my baby cousin, had persuaded the headmistress of the small village school to accept a four-year old. Once there, a few slightly older children adopted me into their gang and I began to discover that life had endless exciting possibilities. And so it was, on a sunny afternoon at the beginning of the Harvest holiday that they stood at our back door asking for me to go and play with them. "Keep together … and don't go too far away!" called my Aunt as we ran down the path, across the road and into the fields where there were trees just waiting to be climbed. The leader of this motley crew was seven year old Barney who stood head and shoulders above the rest of us.

"Single file!" he commanded. "Old Tom Weaver won't cut this until next week. If we jam down his corn he'll be after the lot of us … so take care". Doing as we had been told we made our way along one side of the field concentrating on the narrow rim of grass twixt golden corn and ditch. "Nearly there!" called out Tommy as they arrived at the corner and a nearby five-bar gate. One by one they clambered over. Being the smallest and youngest didn't mean that I needed help, and looking down at the semi-circle of faces, I knew that this was a test of my capabilities within the gang. Somehow, I slithered to the ground wiping my hands on my dress. "Right", Barney winked at me, then issued the next order: "Even though this has been cut, he'll still probably moan like hell if anyone tells him they've seen us here, so keep to the edge … in the next field, there are some cows … and", he paused for effect "and some spiffing trees". "What's a spiffing tree?" I asked. "Dunno, but they'll be good to shin up. You, littl'un, can be our lookout".

Obviously, I was pondering on this accolade or the cruel stubble, rather than judging the width of the grassy border, for one second my eyes were on the ground and the next, I was in agony, catching glimpses of the sky through a canopy of lush, green stinging nettles. I screamed as my feet sank into slime and mud at the bottom of the ditch. Something was tearing at my knee as the vicious nettles pierced my limbs and face. I scrabbled at roots, brambles and anything I could hold that would get me to the surface. Sobbing, I tilted back my head and could just see the line of children, still as statues with expressions of shock etched on their faces. "Please … please …", was all that I could say. And then Tommy shot forward: "Come on, help me you lot … help me get her out". I could see the bow of ribbon on Brenda Goodman's head. It was wobbling as she, too, started to cry. I was bawling my head off as the boys somehow dragged me upwards, and I landed among Tom Weaver's corn stubble with a whack! I must have passed out, because between the five of them they had hauled me into the cornfield where I lay counting ten eyes all anxious and tearful. Someone, Sally I think, muttered: "We're going to be in big trouble 'specially if she's dead". "She's not dead", put in David, with more confidence than I imagine he felt: "She's got a hole in her leg".

My Auntie Flora was pleased that I was not dead, but nearly passed out when she saw the state I was in, and particularly at the trail of blood which followed me: "Here you boys, help me lie her down on that rug. Oh, oh my word, I feel faint". She sat down heavily: "Get Nurse Thaxton quickly. Go on! Quick! Quick! Your little friend will probably die … she's lost gallons of blood". "Crikey", shouted Barney. "She won't be able to come to my party tomorrow if she dies", cried Brenda, as they all ran to get the district nurse. And within minutes, like the Pied Piper, she bustled up the path, bosoms heaving with her shortness of breath: "Go away, you dreadful children!" she admonished. "Haven't you done enough damage to your little friend? Go home the lot of you".

They left and I was subjected to her ministrations of Camomile lotion, Dettol and iodine. When I could cry no more, I fell asleep until, two hours later, my darling Mother arrived home. Horrified that no doctor had been called, she promptly ordered the nurse to do so, while giving her the length of her tongue and in no uncertain terms questioned her abilities.

It was early evening when a handsome, naval doctor hurried in. He took one look at the cavernous hole across my knee and told my Mother and Aunt to hold me down. He had no means of administering anaesthetic, so stitches would have to be put in without. Clearly, this was usual practice in the midst of naval battles, but not in my Aunt's dining room. I kicked and screamed, tore at my Mother's clothing and pummelled my tearful Aunt, who finally shrieked at the third stitch: "Stop! Stop! I can't bear it, it is too cruel". She let go of my legs and wiped her eyes, as the needle and thread flew through the air and the doctor swore barking: "Hospital". He turned to my Mother saying:

"Wrap her in a blanket; hold this bandage tightly. I shall have to take you in my car ... bring a towel. I don't want blood all over the seats. Hurry up woman". And with that, we were whisked into the Jenny Lind Hospital six miles away. Held tightly in my Mother's arms, I had at last been comforted and was totally uncaring of what lay before me - for that half-hour was surely a fool's paradise.

I was unceremoniously snatched from the car by the burly doctor, handed to a porter who laid me on a stretcher, and before we knew it, we had arrived at the Operating Theatre with my breathless Mother running beside me. Doors seemed to open as if by magic, into what I now think to have been an octagonal room of pure white: screens of white cotton; white walls and cupboards. In the middle, beneath an enormous arc of light, an operating table. Three figures in caps and gowns were waiting, as I was gently transferred to the table, fully clothed and unwashed. Pink calamine and yellow iodine covered every inch of visible flesh, but this was clearly acceptable at that time. My Mother was still there holding my hand as something was put over my nose and mouth.

I knew no more until I sleepily awoke to find a large man wearing a tin hat bending over the bed. I remember giving a shrill shriek and a lady in a dark cape and white head-dress touching my hand: "Sweetheart, you're in hospital. We're making your poor leg better, but we've got to hurry, because Norwich is being bombed again and we have to take all the children into the shelter". She looked so kind, I instantly tried to get out of bed to follow her. But she had gone and I had to be carried, along with what seemed like hundreds of other sick children, to spend the remainder of the night on a top bunk listening for bombs, and quietly crying.

After some time, when the crump, crump noises had stopped, the ARP wardens carried us back to the wards and I remember looking up to the waning stars wondering if my Mother would look up to those same stars? (She and my Aunt, cuddling her baby, would have been in the cupboard under the stairs!) From my bed, I could see a large-faced clock and watched its hands slowly move to six o'clock. Hearing a faint squeak, I raised my head. A nurse had been writing at a table; now she was screwing on the top of her pen. Quickly, I shut my eyes as she came over. She smoothed the sheets whispering: "Try to sleep a little, breakfast will come soon". She smiled at me and I loved her. She left the ward on rubber-soled steps and soon the routine of my days of incarceration began.

Those two weeks were the worst of my young life: lumpy, cold porridge; bedpans; blanket baths and other children crying. But most of all I hated the nurses who ripped off my bandages telling me to: "Be a brave little soldier", and pulled off and on scratchy, cotton night-dresses. Someone had sent flowers to remind me of home: cornflowers, buttercups and poppies. But I simply yearned to be there.

"Why don't they come and see me?" I asked the un-smiley nurse. "Grown-ups can visit on Wednesdays, Saturdays and Sundays". I wanted to cry. I felt frightened and cold inside and 'no' I didn't want minced beef and rice pudding ever again in my life!

"Why are those barrage balloons so close to the windows?" I asked the kindly doctor who was unwinding my bandages, one morning. "To keep us safe", he muttered. "Hmm, I think a rusty tin took a great bite out of your knee. You must stay in bed and rest it". "At home?" "No, little one, I want you to stay here until the leg is mended. You may always walk with a limp; the leg may always be stiff, you see". I didn't see. I didn't want to see. "When can I see my Mummy?" "On Saturday, I expect. I want you to get some fresh air and sunshine, so your bed will be taken outside each afternoon. Very soon you shall go home".

Sometimes my Mother would creep up to the railings which bordered Unthank Road, and there, in the shade of the pine trees, where our beds were placed, she would tell me of all the wonderful plans she was making for my return home. Alas, they didn't include my Father who was a prisoner of the Japanese, but wonder of wonders, she had just received the first news for eighteen months that he was still alive. Although I had no recollection of him, I was pleased. But my news, the nice doctor's prognosis, had been mentioned again, just as the smell of beef mince pervaded the building once again.

Even as I left the 'Jenny', using a baby's pushchair, the ghastly aroma followed me; and guess what Aunt Flora had cooked to welcome me home? Shepherd's pie! But soon, very soon, I was up and about rampaging around the countryside on two good legs with a lovely gang of chums who were so glad I wasn't dead.

SEVENTEEN

Rosemary Martin, born 1954

Seventeen, pregnant and homeless. It was difficult then, no free contraception or advice, and in any case we didn't really understand all that stuff in those days. Getting pregnant was something I just never thought would happen to me!

But there I was, seventeen and expecting a baby. I was still with my boyfriend, but obviously, when Mum and Dad found out – well, that was it - I was a disgrace to the family and they just couldn't bear what the neighbours would say. So I had to leave my family home, with nowhere to go.

After spending a week with a friend, my partner and I found a two up two down house on Barn Road. No bathroom, no hot water and a shared toilet outside. It was partly furnished - but it was all horrible furniture and I really didn't fancy the bed - but there were no options. We managed to get a few pieces together, but not much, as I had to give up work because I was quite poorly with my pregnancy and there was no sick pay to be had. My partner's money was all that was coming into the house and there just wasn't enough money to go round - what with rent, food and utility bills.

The bed was so lumpy and uncomfortable and we only had three blankets and an eiderdown. It was winter and very cold, and being in my condition I often had to get up in the night to go outside to the toilet. So down I would go, open the backdoor and out into the yard. The door to the toilet had a gap at the top and one at the bottom. It was so, so cold!

My partner was not the best of people, and each night after work he would go with his mates to the pub until all hours. He would then come home drunk, often knocking me around for no particular reason, expecting me to get food for him at that time of night.

A bath was a rare event as we had no bathroom and could not afford to buy a tin bath. The woman next door was sometimes kind enough to let me use her bathwater once she and her husband had finished with it, which felt like a real blessing at the time. Every morning I had to boil a kettle to be able to have a strip down wash. I washed all my clothes and linen by hand and borrowed my neighbour's spin dryer to get out the worst of the water so that the laundry wouldn't drip everywhere. Then of course, if the weather was bad and it couldn't go on the line, it would come indoors to dry near the fire - if we could afford the coal to burn (which was a real luxury).

It all sounds quite awful now, but it's just the way things were forty years ago if you were poor. There wasn't the help that you get now from the Government, and no Primark, QD or Poundland where you can buy the everyday necessities quite cheaply today. It was so difficult – a constant struggle to keep my head above water and survive!

But I did survive, thank goodness. Sadly, I lost my son at birth and before long split up from my boyfriend (which was ultimately a blessing) and I am here today to tell the story.

I now thank God everyday for what I have - a lovely flat, warmth, plenty of food on the table, a lovely daughter, two beautiful grand children and my happiness – which money could never buy.

LIVINGSTONE CATS

Helen Massy, born 1958

From 1996 until 2009 I lived in Livingstone Street, Norwich and saw many changes. These were often marked by the appearance of a new cat in my garden - or its disappearance some time later.

I became fond of these cats: Morag, Bessie and Bertie, Stone, Boss Cat, Smaug, Caspar, and the ginger Tom. On hot summer afternoons, we would bask in the sun in my back garden in peaceful companionship.

Boss Cat commandeered number 13 and seemed to be resident there, when I first moved into the Street. The students in the house fed him - I guess others did too - he was a fair size.

I wasn't keen on him at first, but over the years, that changed. Sometimes he joined me when I sat in the garden and I began to appreciate his character and company. One day, I noticed that he had developed a wheeze and had difficulty breathing. Soon after, he was simply not there anymore.

My favourite cat was Morag, next-door at number 11. She was so devoted to her owner that she wailed incessantly while he was away. His imminent return caused her to scrabble excitedly at the fence with her claws and she only calmed down once he had arrived.

Even when suffering from throat cancer and arthritic stiffness, she was athletic. She frequently leapt up and down the full-size fence or walked delicately along the top. My attempts to hug or stroke her were often rejected with teeth and claws, albeit gently used as a warning - she preferred to be dignified.

Morag still holds a place in my heart and on numerous photographs. She died of cancer - the vet put her down when she became too weak and could no longer eat.

Smaug found his way into the garden from two streets away. He hid in a nearby dilapidated greenhouse at night. We became good friends for two or three days. Then my neighbour told me that the owners had called by to try and catch him.

The following day, I lured him into the house and closed the back door behind him. He was still exploring the place when his owners came to take him home. All went smoothly and six weeks later I visited him and saw that he had settled back contentedly.

Bertie and Bessie, two black cats, used to stalk insects - following their movements with rapt attention. One afternoon, I squatted by them and spent a happy fifteen minutes watching some bees at work.

When the cats were about, clipping the lawn was hazardous. They came so close to the shears that I had to feign anger so that they would flee. It was soon forgotten, until the day I accidently closed the shears on Bertie's paw. From then on, he was more cautious.

The ginger Tom, friendly and playful as a kitten, became aloof over time. He was king of the garden and also an agile climber, so birds avoided the plum tree and foraged elsewhere for food. I admired him and let him stalk past me as he chose.

Early one morning, a black kitten with wide frightened eyes jumped onto the narrow window sill of the dining room. He meowed pitifully and I went outside to comfort him. When he had calmed down a little, I looked at the ring tag on his collar and noted the telephone number and his name - Caspar. I dialled the number and a woman replied. She told me that he lived at number 19 - four doors away, and came round to fetch him.

Caspar grew to be a sleek confident cat, at ease with his place in the back garden community of cats. He was never intimidated, though not really a fighter. His well-being was often the topic of conversation with his owners, as well as work and family.

Stone was demure and poised, self-contained. Tortoiseshell in colour, she'd curl up next to the flints in my rockery, which caught the heat of the day. Motionless except for the movement of her breath or the flicker of an ear or tail, she was a real 'living stone'. She gave meaning to the name of the street and the back garden life there. Shortly before I moved house, I noticed her absence.

Now, living elsewhere, I sometimes think of my feline friends and wonder how their lives might be. No doubt cats (and their owners) still come and go. The generations and tales of change on Livingstone Street continue.

A TONIC AND TOOTHPASTE TALE

Merryl Burton, born 1951

At the age of fifteen, I left school and got a job working at Wincarnis on Barn Road. They bottled sherry and also made the famous tonic wine Wincarnis Red and a special fortified one called Wincarnis Gold, which had beef extract in it. The factory was very noisy with all the belts and bottles rattling. I was set to work on the 'foiling': all the bottles had silver foil or gold foil round the necks and it was applied by hand and was rubbed down - quite an art - which I did not possess, so I was moved to bottling sherry. I hated the smell but I loved the job. We had to cork and label the bottles by hand in the early days. Later it was done by machine. After a while I became friendly with an old man called Jack. He had the Reindeer Pub on the Dereham Road and used to come up to the factory to 'lay down bottles'. We worked in the cellars: there were 'bins' where the sherry and wine were stored. Row upon row, rack upon rack, and year by year, labelled and stored and turned regularly by me and Jack.

I was quite a tomboy and lived in jeans. We had our yearly dinner dance coming up and he said his greatest wish was to see me as a girl. He bought me my first pair of stockings. So I got a dress and had my hair done in the latest Mary Quant style and went to the dance. I felt like Cinderella. He was a lovely kind old man and was so pleased that I looked like a woman. He treated me like a daughter and was so proud of the way I looked.

At Christmas the chief blender of spirits used to get all the dregs from the bottoms of the barrels and make a batch of what was called

Special Blended. All the workers were allowed three bottles each; it was very strong. I used to go to work on my bicycle - it had a basket on the front and I had been paying weekly for some special sherry glasses

that the firm used to sell in sets of six for my mother for Christmas. It was my first Christmas at work and as I came into the yard with my bike, my Special Blended and my glasses ... you can guess what happened: I dropped my bike and lost my mother's present and the wine all smashed! Reggie Raynor saw what happened and came to my rescue; he got me a dozen glasses and six bottles of Special Blended and told me to stop crying and to have a good Christmas. I never forgot his kindness to me. We had a wonderful Christmas.

Later in the year I was put to work in the Mouthwash and Toothpaste Factory which was another part of Wincarnis. They made Odol Mouthwash and Punch and Judy Toothpaste. I hated it! The mouthwash was terrible stuff; it took the colour from your clothes and after a week or two your shoes would fall apart and the soles would fall off the uppers.

I was only there for about a month, then I was moved to the last department - the "Vitacup" Factory where a malted drink, similar to Horlicks, was made in big stone vats which turned it into granules like coffee. It was put into tins by machine and we had to put the lids on and make sure the labels were straight. They were a lovely lot of girls and we all used to sing along to the factory music of the time - being a child of the sixties we had the Beatles, the Rolling Stones, the Kinks and other famous bands.

I only worked there for two years. I met my husband Bob at sixteen and got married on Christmas Eve 1968 aged seventeen years. We were happy for thirty-eight years when he sadly died at the age of fifty-six. But I never forgot working at Wincarnis. It was a worldwide name: Wincarnis Tonic Wine and Punch and Judy Toothpaste. I am the oldest of eight children and they all enjoyed brushing their teeth with the toothpaste which tasted like fruit salad sweets - so Mum was glad about that!

Reflections on a Changing City

Vera Grimwood, born 1928

Norwich city is a changing place,
Our memories leaving a fading trace
Of all that's been through many a year:
The essence of it is recorded here.

Shopping centres have changed a lot;
Gone are most of out local shops,
All our factories that used to be:
Florida Shoes, Swan Laundry,
Good old Nestles Chocolate Factory.

The old city walls still stand astride
But shopping malls are built beside.
On Chapelfield we'd dance a Monday night away:
Around the bandstand our dresses swayed.

The Yards, our homes, mostly pulled down:

Hooks Yard where I lived when young -

On a nail our bath tub hung.

The cattle would come down Duke's Street

The drovers taking them to market, then meet

To have a pint at the end of the day.

Now Yards and shops have gone away.

Shoe factories: Howlett's and White's, and Whitten

Most of them are gone, but none forgotten.

In St Benedict's, two great stores:

One called Jarvice's, one called Moore's

They never had no counter tills

But tubes to place the cash to pay the bills;

Up the chute to the office girls neat

Back down again with change and receipt.

Samson and Hercules on Saturday night

We enjoyed ourselves without a fight.

Rock and Roll was great to watch:

Tight trousers and white Bobby Sox.

In the war time I went to school:

First at St Augustine's, then Angel Road.

Air Raid shelters dug deep in the grounds

When the sirens sounded, swift safety we found.

We grew our fruit and veg in gardens then

Not pre-packed until the dates end.

Picture Houses that used to be:

The Regent Electric, and Sixpenny Rush on Saturday.

The horse and cart packed with bags of coal

To keep the home fires burning when we were cold.

Fun was fun: we grew up poor

But all were welcome through our doors.

We weren't afraid to welcome them in

As robbery then was an unlikely sin.

At fourteen I worked at Read's Flour Mills

Wages, seven and sixpence for my time and my skills,

I'd buy Mum a bunch of flowers, and still I might

Go down the Samson on Saturday night.

The Dutch boats sailed down riverside

Read's Flour Mill, King Street:
Illustration based on a Bridewell Museum (NCC) image

Packed with sacks of flour, their sails wide;

Watching from the factory window,

I waved them good luck as they'd go.

Now I have got a great deal older

Living in sheltered housing and getting bolder!

I love my bungalow where I live

And there's always somebody ready to give.

Coffee mornings, bring a light,

Fish and chips once a fortnight,

Line dancing for my nights out

Instead of all the twists and shouts.

As for transport, we're doing fine

The bus passes came in super time -

To travel to the city and around:

There is some good in the modern, I've found.

Ups and down I've had a few

But smooth it was not meant to be, I knew.

I brought up a family of nine –

A well earned rest now, I'm doing fine.

INEBRIATE KATIE

Sheila Nursey, born 1926

It was a thing of the past, a day out during the War, when a workmate, whose husband had left her with two young children to bring up, informed me that her local pub had organised a day out. As her only pleasure was usually a glass of stout with the Ladies' Dart's Team on Friday nights, this was a great treat. It was also to celebrate, as our men were advancing on all fronts in the Second World War.

It was a beautiful day. As I walked towards the Pub's forecourt a group of ladies of all shapes and sizes greeted me. A very tall one - I suddenly had a vision of carrot coloured hair, a very short skirt, bright red winkle picker shoes, a cigarette, dangling from her ruby red lips: "I'm Joan, chairwoman of the Ladies' Dart's Team". Amidst all the introductions, suddenly Joan's voice, shouted: "Where's Katie?" Around the corner of the pub came Katie. An exclamation of disgust and surprise came from Joan and several of the women. "She's already been drinking". "She's a disgrace to the human species". Katie's figure was encased in a crepe dechine dress, which had shrunk two sizes small for her fat little figure. A battered straw hat hung precariously over one side of her head. Her fat little feet were encased in plastic strip sandals and several of the strips were flopping on the floor. She shouted: "Here I am".

At the same time a terrible rattling noise came within earshot, sounding like a load of old tin cans: our coach came round the corner. Cat calls came from the group: "Where did you get the old tin can, it's full of rust?" A little man jumped out of the rusting door, touching his filthy cheesecutter cap: "Name's Bertie ma'am". Joan's impatient voice: "Well, help me to get these two crates of stout into the bus". A shout from Bertie: "Ladies, be careful to step over the hole in the floor boards".

Katie immediately sat near the crates of stout. Joan pointed her finger at me: "You and Phyllis sit near Katie; see she don't help herself to the stout". At the same time she was demanding to know where Bertie got the old bone shaker from. "The Yanks found it in a barn; they done it up for me and put petrol in. Well, one good turn deserves another, I told them where all the girls go dancing".

We all settled comfortably in our seats hoping for a nice day out. It was just outside Loddon, near Lord Langley's Park when a shout went up from Katie: "Stop! Stop! I need the toilet". Bertie's voice shouted in anger: "You'll have to wait; can't stop now". Joan stamped down the gangway, looking at Katie's sprawled-out figure, her crepe dechine dress raised above her thighs showing her pink silk knickers. "You can't afford silk knickers". "Got them at Boy Scouts' jumble", was Katie's answer. Bertie stopped the bus wagging his finger uncontrollably at Katie. His face was red with anger: "Right. Down the ditch; up into the woods". Ten minutes passed and no Katie. Phyllis and I volunteered to go and look for her.

The further we went into the woods, the more frightening it became. The smell of rotting leaves and fungi was nauseating; overgrown brambles and nettles tore at our legs. The slivers of sunlight through the trees had gone and our shouts were of no avail. Katie had just disappeared. We ran from the woods, like terrified rabbits shouting: "We can't find her". Bertie took hold of the situation: "Right, girls". Arming himself with a tree branch: "Get yourselves a lump of wood and follow me".

We must have looked a peculiar sight: a group of mature ladies with lumps of wood in our hands, in crocodile line, tramping behind a tiny little man, all shouting for Katie. The further we went in, the darker and more desolate it got. We were really scared. Bertie was whispering: "Shush, I heard something". There it was again, a woman's high-pitched laugh. Suddenly we were confronted by an old dilapidated shed. Bertie raised his branch and at the same time grabbed the door of the old shed, which fell off its hinges. Shock and bewilderment was on all our faces, for there sat Katie on the knees of the funniest little man I'd ever seen. His deerstalker hat cocked on one side, his little legs encased in tight breeches, his pot belly popping all the buttons.

"Come out", shouted Bertie. Katie replied in an incoherent voice: "No, I don't want to, I'm staying here". Deerstalker stood up: "You heard what the lady said". Without another word he cocked a rifle at our heads. "Clear off out my woods". I think we all beat any marathon race records in a few split seconds as we rushed to leave the wood and trooped back to the bus.

Bertie pulled up at the nearest Police Station, explaining what had happened to the elderly desk Sergeant. "Well now, since the lady in question, is over sixty, she ought to know her own mind". Bertie was dismissed with a wave of the Sergeant's hand. We all made our way home. Our very rare day out had been a disappointing one, but nonetheless, quite exciting.

Some weeks later, Katie had been missing for three weeks. The landlord of the pub made enquiries. Apparently Katie was now working as a housekeeper and was about to marry Lord Langley's gamekeeper!

BISHOPGATE REMEMBERED

Joan Smith, born 1925

When my parents first brought me to live in Bishopgate I was just six weeks old. Bishopgate at that time was a mixed and thriving thoroughfare sheltered by the Cathedral Close on one side and the River Wensum slowly meandering round the other. Bishop Bridge had once been the only way over the water into the city.

On the North side there were four terraces at right angles from the street, namely Goldsworth Buildings, Bull Square, Balaclava and Inkermen Terrace. Further along the street stands The Great Hospital, affectionately known at that time as 'The Old Man's Hospital'. Then round the bend there is the Adam and Eve (reputedly the oldest Public House in Norwich). As we continue round a few more cottages, there were the Gas Works. Flames resembling a breathing dragon belched day and night from this edifice fed by a tall upright revolving structure which carried the coal up high and then tipped it into the furnace below. Children would be sent with their barrows to collect cheap coke and also to inhale the tarring fumes their parents believed would ease all manner of chest complaints.

At the end of each terrace, small businesses survived. Amongst these were: The Red Lion Public House; Hales Furniture removers (later a hairdressers); a post office; two funeral directors; two grocers; a cobblers; and a further pub - The Marquis of Granby. Each made a living of sorts. All these properties at that time were rented out by the Great Hospital Trustees.

The South side of the road was more affluent with much larger and grander houses which had been built on land leased out by the Cathedral Diocese. Then there was a Kindergarten School (now the Norwich School Lower Form) and finally the grounds to the Bishop's Palace.

I was six months old when my parents took 'rooms' at my Great Aunt's at 10 Inkerman Terrace whilst they waited for a cottage of their own - which they soon moved into at 14 Balaclava Terrace. We lived there very happily until I was eleven years old. As these were only two bed-roomed cottages I shared my bedroom with my brother (seven years my senior) with just a blanket strung across the room for privacy. Once, however, I reached eleven years of age, it was mandatory to have a separate bedroom and we were moved to a council house in Lakenham. My mother hated it and could not wait to get back to Bishopgate. So eighteen months later we returned to No. 3 Inkerman

Terrace where we solved the sleeping problem by my brother sleeping downstairs in the front room.

These were happy years with all the children from the area attending Thorpe Hamlet School. There was, however, a great deal of unemployment, or worse still, 'short time', when there was only enough work for a few hours a day. If you were unemployed you could draw the 'dole' but you only had to have two hour's work to lose this benefit. We were quite a poor family but were considered well-off because my father, although poorly paid, was never out of work and my mother could always pay the bills and rent, and buy coal. When my father retired after forty-two years' service at 'Fitt Bros' it was too late for a firm's pension, so he was presented with a watch and twenty-five pounds. I remember saying to him "I did think they could have given you at least ten shillings a week". He replied: "My girl, I had forty-two years' employment.

When the war started in 1939 many of our young men were drafted into the Royal Norfolk Regiment and lots of them later spent years in Japanese hands. Here at home we had soldiers billeted on us and spent considerable time in the brick built shelters (the land here was too marshy for Andersons) waiting for the 'All clear' to sound. German planes would come in over the East Coast en route to the Midlands and we had to sit and wait for them to return. We had, of course, considerable damage in Norwich especially with the Baedeker Raids and the first incendiary bombs dropped on English towns and cities. Bishopgate, however, was lucky, despite the flames from the gas works drawing attention to the area. Bombs fell on the grammar school field and the Hospital meadow, knocking out the windows and bringing down the ceilings; but "Thank God" there were no casualties.

On my wedding day, which had been planned for 8th May 1945 at the Parish Church of St Helen's, the war ended and the Government declared a forty-eight hour holiday for everybody. Consequently the florist, photographer, wedding cars and organist all failed to turn up.

Even my wedding reception was cancelled. My poor mother flew round like a headless chicken. This marriage unfortunately was not to last, but that is another story.

Eventually I married again and at twenty-five years of age left the street for the first time, moving only as far away as Magdalen Street. So I was always walking 'round the walls' to visit my parents, who later moved into the Great Hospital. That is where I am now – in a beautiful flat at St Helen's House, which stands within the perimeter of the Hospital grounds. This House was designed, built and lived in by Thomas Ivory in 1756. Later it was to become a private hotel, then a nursing home and was finally converted by the Great Hospital into eight roomy flats. All those years ago when I lived in the small 'two up, two down' cottage, little did I imagine that I would finish up living in the Grand House up the street. This is one happy chicken come home to roost!

TEENAGE YEARS: COURTING AND STARTING WORK

John Riseborough, born 1937

One Saturday a friend suggested we go to a meeting at the hall in Surrey Street that had been advertised on the board at the City Technical College. So we went, and I have no recollection at all of the meeting except that my friend was chatting up the two girls in the seats in front of us.

The girl Peter selected was very short for him and her name was Jeannie. The other was called Sheila. They both lived in Hethersett and had to catch the last bus at Surrey Street Bus Station at about 10:30. So Peter made arrangements to meet them at Hethersett Church the next day, after Evensong. He was very persistent, old Peter, so I finished up catching the bus with him on the Sunday to meet these girls. We arrived in Hethersett in time to attend the Evensong at Hethersett Church where both the girls were in the choir, and afterwards we walked them home very slowly. Jean lived at the corner of Melton Road and Mill Road and we lingered there for a time before I walked Sheila home to New Road, where I was invited in to meet her parents.

When it was time for me to catch the bus Sheila came with me to the end of New Road on the A11, pushing her bike for her return journey. When the bus loomed close by, she wrapped her arms around my neck and gave me my first real, on the mouth, kiss! We were lit up in the bus headlights and when I boarded the bus I wanted the world to open up and swallow me. I imagine my face was scarlet: it felt as if it was on fire. For two pins I would have walked home, I was so embarrassed. But I went back again for more … and more … and more.

I courted her for two and a half years, either biking to Hethersett or, when the weather was too bad, walking there and back.

In the autumn of 1953 I sat an entrance exam for Laurence & Scott's and failed. At least, I never heard that I had passed. I also applied for an engineering apprenticeship in the Royal Navy and was told I'd missed the boat! The age limit was fifteen and I was now over sixteen.

I was still doing a paper round because I needed the cash, and I also managed to land a temporary Christmas job at the GPO as a telegram boy. I had to register with the Employment Exchange and pay National Insurance and tax on my earnings, but I still got a little cash for Christmas presents. Being a telegram boy was quite exciting in a way because mostly we 'temps' were given the 'good news' messages and the regular telegram boys, who rode BSA Bantam motorbikes, got the 'bad news' deliveries. The job entailed rather a lot of sitting around waiting for work, and we eventually realised it was silly to rush back to the office because the next job would go to somebody else anyway.

In June 1954 I sat my GCE exams and failed in all except English language. I hated examinations because my brains always seemed to desert me when I needed them. But I did manage to get a job, by default I suppose and this is how...

An old pal, Simon, had got a job working for the Norfolk News Company in March. He was taken on as an adult apprentice working in the foundry. He was the Scoutmaster of the Ranworth Troop and when he was taking them to California (no, the one near Caister) for a summer camp he asked me to go along as an assistant.

The campsite was in a field next to the disused railway lines. The field was owned by a little old gentleman. There was a small barn there and we were really grateful it was available because on the Saturday night the heavens opened and we were nearly washed away. Simon and I and the senior scouts managed to get everybody into the barn before any lasting damage was done, with all their bedding and dry clothes. It rained all night and in the morning the field looked a sorry mess! But as is usual with British weather, the sun shone the next day and everywhere dried out, so we carried on as normal.

We had some visitors on the Sunday, one of whom was Simon's boss, a Mr Taylor. I had been teaching some scouts how to do rope splicing and lashings and he asked me if I had a job to go to when I finished at the City College. I told him I hadn't, and explained about the Navy and the Laurence & Scott's exam. He told me that if I was interested, he would give me a job in his Department. I was not only 'interested' - I was delighted!

An interview was arranged with Mr Young the General Manager and I was offered an apprenticeship in either the foundry or the reading room, whichever I preferred. The snag with the reading room was that I would have to begin working on the night shift whereas the foundry was a day job, at least until I finished my apprenticeship. So I naturally took the job in the foundry.

Each apprentice was allocated to a Journeyman and worked with him as a team, learning his way of doing things. I became apprentice No 4 with Jimmy Webb, Tony Barker and Simon Everard above me. That meant I had to get the coffee every morning at 10:00 and the tea every afternoon at 3:15, or as soon as the County Edition was put to bed.

The canteen was upstairs in a little building on the back of Suckling House and the lady who dispensed the refreshments was 'Auntie Glad'. She took great care of her 'Boys' and always made sure we got good milky coffee with plenty of sugar. There were ten mugs on the tray and the spoon was on a little bit of lavatory chain, soldered to the tray.

In 1955 a new apprentice started. He was a Scotsman whose father was a friend of Mr Young. Ian was older than me and had finished his National Service. His home was in Inverness and both he and his brother, Dave, came to work at the Norfolk News Company. He objected to being the 'tea boy' so we had to share the job on alternate weeks.

Ian discovered Looses shop in Magdalen Street and he bought a mug there. They told him it was 'unbreakable'. It was made of Melaware. To demonstrate its indestructibility he tossed it up in the air and let it fall to the concrete floor, whereupon it shattered into a thousand pieces. He took it back and got a new one.

The canteen served very good midday meals at extremely reasonable prices, so I always dined there. Wednesday was always fish and chip day and when they made shepherd's pie with gravy there were chips too, if anyone wanted them.

My first day at work was on August 4th which was the Bank Holiday Monday in those days. The papers were always very small on Bank Holidays so we seemed to spend a lot of time just waiting about for something to happen. Everybody was paid extra on Bank Holidays, except me. I earned £3: 06d a week for my first year and had annual increments of a percentage of the journeyman's pay thereafter. I also had to join the Union, which horrified my Dad. I became a member of the National Association of Electrotypers and Stereotypers.

Their meetings were always held on Sunday Mornings in a room above the Festival House Pub in St Andrews Street. A lot of members came from Jarrold's in Norwich, Clay's of Bungay and Clowes of Beccles, as well as a few from Cox & Wyman in Fakenham.

My new job entailed making the printing plates for printing the EDP, EEN, the Norfolk News Series and the Pink-Un. These plates each weighed at least 45lbs and were cast from an alloy of lead (60%), tin (5%) and antimony (35%) in a curved shape to fit round the cylinders of the printing press.

The pages were made up in a flat form in the composing room and then came to the stereo department on a trolley to be moulded into a flat sheet of thick card that was called a 'flong'. This 'flong' was then dried and prepared for the casting process. Then it was inserted into a semi-circular casting box and molten lead was poured into it. The machine that cast the plates was called a Pony Autoplate that cut and trimmed the plate to the required length and thickness. Then the plate was manhandled onto the press cylinders in pairs where the continuous sheet of paper was threaded between the rollers to print the paper.

The best printing machine when I began work was a Foster press, made in about 1939, which could print about 40,000 copies an hour at full belt. There was another very old press which was affectionately called the 'Trundler' which might manage about 15,000 copies an hour if the wind was right! It must have been a Victorian antique in

1954 but when the new Hoe-Crabtree press was installed in 1955 the 'Trundler' was sold to an African country along with one of the Pony Autoplate machines to serve out the rest of its days. I'll bet it's still going now, 50 years later! Our old 'pony' machines were replaced by new 'Junior Autoplate' machines.

We had to work on Saturdays to print the Evening News and the Pink 'Un, the local sports paper, so I had to give up my place in the rugby team. But now I had other interests and I kept fit by biking out to Hethersett and back several nights a week.

One rather amusing episode happened just before work started on the new office building in Redwell Street. In the days of the London Street Office we had a back door that came out into Redwell Street, next to Todhouse Raynard the tailors. Just next door to them was the City Arms public house. On a Saturday, in the wait between the Evening News finishing and the Pink 'Un beginning, it was customary for some of the 'Gentlemen of the foundry' to adjourn to the City Arms for some swift refreshment. They didn't all go by any means, and apprentices were not exactly encouraged to imbibe. Ted was the most ardent worshipper of the demon ale and he could put it away wholesale. So, one Saturday he was the first in, as usual, to order his pint. There was already a pint tankard on the bar and Ted thought the landlord had pulled it as he arrived and it was his. He picked it up and just poured it down his throat without swallowing, as he always did with his first one. In micro-seconds it came right back up again.

"What the heck have you done to the beer?" he demanded of the barman.

"What beer?" asked the barman indignantly.

"Well that pint tasted awful", complained Ted.

"It should have", said the barman: "It's pipe cleaning fluid, you idiot. I've just finished flushing out the pipes to the cellar".

Ted came to work from Loddon on a little motor bike and one Saturday morning, a rather bright sunny day, he arrived soaking wet. Somebody asked him if it was raining, but it transpired that he was riding behind a cattle float and a cow had pee'ed out of the side, so Ted copped the lot in the slipstream.

Now that I was earning real wages I decided to buy myself a decent bike; I had been using Dad's more or less non-stop for years. I selected a brand-new Raleigh Sports model from Mr Bingham's shop on Unthank Road and paid £24 at 10/- a week hire-purchase. I still have the little paying record card that shows I never missed a payment. I loved that bike and when I finally sold it in about 1985 I only got £5. It had a little Tennis Racquet clip on the front forks in which I used, in later years, to carry my garden fork to the allotments on Cromer Road.

I could also afford to take my girlfriend to the pictures on a Saturday night, or to a dance. The dancing lessons I went to when I was about fourteen years old were now coming in handy. I had attended lessons at Eileen Page's school of dance in Elm Hill. They cost 2/6 per session and we were taught the waltz, quickstep and samba. They started on the foxtrot, but I stopped going soon after.

In the summer of 1955 I had a letter from 'the Queen' telling me to report to Martineau House in Colegate for a medical examination for National Service. I duly turned up and was examined, poked and prodded all over. The doctor who listened to my heart and measured my blood pressure wasn't happy with what he heard and consulted another doctor who also had a listen. Then they sent me away with instructions to return the following week.

At work they told me I could have a deferment until I had finished my apprenticeship in five years time, so I applied to defer my call-up for five years. It was duly granted, but I still had to go for the medical again. This time I was declared A1 fit for service. They also asked me if I had any preference for any of the services. I requested to be sent

61

to the Royal Navy because I had been on a ship once before, when I went to France, so I was half trained already! They couldn't have been listening - I was drafted into the RAF.

In September Sheila went to live in a place called Harvington, near Evesham in Worcestershire. I used to have to ring her from a call box once a week by asking the operator for a trunk call and waiting to be connected and then putting in the pennies as ordered by the operator.

Now I was without a girlfriend and all lonely. Jock reckoned I would be best advised to cancel my deferment and do my National Service now. If I waited until I finished my apprenticeship I would go from full man's pay down to 28/- a week, and that didn't make good sense. So I requested my deferment be cancelled and waited for the Queen to send for me, which She did.

Night-time
in Norridge

Barry Prime, born 1938

Back in the nineteen-fifties and sixties I was an avid filmgoer, visiting the cinema at least once a week. The places I went in order to do this included Stalham, North Walsham, Great Yarmouth and of course, Norwich. I was a country boy from the wilds of Stalham, so the big city was quite a revelation to me. In those days Norwich had a good selection of picture houses; a good variety too. The following are the ones I have frequented, some of them regularly and some just once or twice.

There was the ABC on Prince of Wales Road, the Odeon on Botolph Street, Theatre DeLuxe on St. Andrew's Street, Mayfair on Magdalen Street, the Regal and the Ritz - I always get mixed up with these two, though I think the Regal was situated where J. D. Wetherspoon's is now at the Grapes Hill end of Dereham Road and The Ritz much further out on that road, past where The Norwood Rooms Dance Hall used to be. I frequented the Carlton, later called The Gaumont on All Saints' Green (now a bingo hall), spending most of my time there with my wife-to-be, Irene. To complete the 'picture' there was The Haymarket on - well - the Haymarket, replaced now by Top Shop. The Carlton was our favourite because we usually had to run for our respective buses - 5A to Stalham and 9A to Coltishall - and this cinema was the closest to the Surrey Street Bus Station.

These cinemas all had the typical features that are remembered with affection: neatly uniformed usherettes to halve our tickets and show us, by torchlight, to the correctly priced seating; a lady with a large tray, which she had to support with a strap around her neck. Her job was to sell ice creams in little round tubs with wooden spoons to dip in, and Kia-Ora orange juice, with straws we made disgusting sounds with as the container emptied. .

In those days they presented us with two films, one an A and the other a B, the B usually being a half hour long pseudo documentary about the police or a short western. There was also a trailer of next week's films and the Movietone or Pathe News. Oh, and of course, the Pearl and Dean adverts. You could go in at any time, staying until the film came round again to where you had come in. But if you did this you would have to put up with the smell of 'Flit' that they sprayed in order not to be called a flea-pit. One of the above named cinemas did have this reputation, but I won't identify it (save to say its name rhymed with nits).

Another good night out in the early sixties was to be had in Exchange Street, albeit with none of the comforts you expect nowadays. Our own Jarrold's Department Store, plus their Office Equipment Shop dominate one side of that street now, but in my younger days this was the scene of my second date with Irene. The first date was far more conventional - The Odeon Cinema, but the second was of her choice. It was in the Corn Exchange Hall, after which Exchange Street was named, to watch, and in the case of some of the female audience, to take part in, the events staged there. Sitting on uncomfortable auctioneers' desks and in this draughty hall we would watch the likes of Messrs Mick McManus, Jackie Pallo and Billy Two Rivers performing their showbiz type roles in something called Wrestling. I am certain that if some of the throws and slams to the canvas were bona fide, there would have been serious injuries and even fatalities. But the women seemed to think they were real, and sometimes attacked the 'villains' with their handbags or any other suitable weapon.

On Agricultural Hall Plain, Anglia Television still holds sway. One of the buildings there used to be The Post Office and I must confess that it was the scene of one of my faux pas. I had started to date a young lady from my works and in this instance she had arranged for us to start our night out by meeting at the 'Norwich Post Office'. Arriving in Norwich by bus, and alighting at the bus station in Surrey Street, she naturally meant the nearer post office in Queen's Road, situated roughly where the RSPCA shop is now. I thought she meant the other one, as I believed it was the main one. Consequently, we never met that day. I am ashamed to add that when she found out that, by sheer accident, I bumped into another female acquaintance and went to the pictures with her, we never met again.

On the corner of Red Lion Street and Farmer's Avenue, opposite Debenhams, there is a building which has changed ownership quite a few times over the years. Its last long-term resident was The Halifax Building Society, but in the times I am recalling, it housed The Coach and Horses Pub, which, together with The Lamb and The Boar's Head in the vicinity, was a favourite watering hole of my brothers, my mates and me. My first entry into the 'Coach' was with my brother Mike, who shall remain nameless. As we made our way through the spacious but well-packed room, Mike spotted someone that he knew, or thought he did, so he left me in order to approach him. I must add at this juncture that Mike usually wore glasses, but took them off when going out on a Saturday night. In those days fewer people wore specs, and he thought they would be off-putting to girls. Anyway, he got as near as a few feet from this familiar person, but then stopped, embarrassed, and turned back immediately. He had advanced on the pub's large wall mirror and confronted himself.

A favourite place for Irene and I to have a drink and a bite to eat, especially after a visit to the Regent Cinema (later the ABC), was The Wimpy Bar on the opposite side of Prince of Wales Road. It was quite a 'with-it' venue in those days, with its espresso coffee and beef burgers. Until then we had frequented such places as Lyons Corner Tea Houses, one of them on Gentleman's Walk, or ordinary check-patterned-plastic-table-clothed restaurants. There were no nightclubs around then - they hadn't been invented in Norwich at that time. Nor were there any ethnic restaurants - unless you counted Valori's Chip Shop.

65

I can remember a couple of the shops down Prince of Wales Road. One was Wilmott's, where you could buy such disparate things as a bicycle or a gramophone record. You could have the luxury of listening to the record that you fancied buying, in a booth, but I'm pretty sure that they wouldn't let you test ride the bikes prior to purchasing.

The other shop was Wallace King's Furniture Store and the attraction of this on a night out in Norwich, before or after a show, was that they had a convenient U-shaped arcade in which a young couple could shelter in inclement weather and cuddle sans self consciousness - and at no cost.

These are my memories of nights out in the fifties and sixties. You will note that I have not made mention of dance halls such as the Samson and Hercules, The Gala and The Grosvenor and that's for a good reason. I had two left feet, nay, they were blocks of lead, and I would doubtlessly have been charged with cruelty if let loose on a dance floor. Worse still, I boycotted the theatres - Royal, Hippodrome and Maddermarket, as I mistakenly thought they were for snobs.

IN THE BEGINNING
THERE WAS MATRON
Bee Norfolk, born 1934

So this was it, our first day on the ward and treating real patients. It was August 1952, only four years after the NHS had begun. It was a good time to be in nursing.

I had arrived at the Norfolk and Norwich Hospital, St Stephens Road, three months previously, to start my three-year training to become a State Registered Nurse. Those first three months I had spent in PTS (Preliminary Training School) learning how to make a bed and at the same time preserve the patient's modesty. However that was with one of our colleagues playing the patient. Therefore there were no drips in arms, or nasal feeds, not to mention abdominal sutures to hinder the movements. Neither were there tubes running from various parts of the patient's anatomy to bottles on the floor - some red, some green, yellow, or even black, all designed to trip you up or stub your toe. We had also injected oranges with water, but trust me the real thing was something else, possessing eyes and a voice!

Our uniforms were made to measure, in the sewing room, where an army of seamstresses measured us. We had to kneel on the ground to get the length right. Our aprons were pristine white and starched, matching our caps. This gave us an air of cleanliness and authority that I do not see today. Each year a stripe was added to our sleeve to denote how long we had been in training and of course, after finals, when one became a qualified nurse, the blue belt and silver buckle told the world that you had passed.

In our three months in school we digested a lot about anatomy and physiology. To aid us we had a once-live skeleton who, in our innocence, we named James, although, as we learned a little more anatomy, it dawned upon us that James once walked this earth as Jemima. Plastic bones took over from there on. Things were already changing.

My first ward placement, Orthopaedics of the male category, brought a mixture of excitement, fear and hope. Early morning, we gathered around the table situated in the centre of the ward, to hear the night nurse's report. She went through the entire patient list, bed-by-bed, stating which drugs the patient had been given and what sort of a night he had had. I listened intently, pleased when I could relate to any word which made me feel less alien to this new world I was entering. Then we dispersed to our various duties. I tried not to look too inexperienced, which, I kidded myself, I accomplished until someone on the open air balcony said: "Nurse, please may I have a bed pan?" I smiled sweetly and nodded. Now, where on earth was the sluice on this ward? I was not averse to handling bedpans if I could only find them! To add to my dilemma this patient was on a boarded bed, sectioned underneath, so I stood somewhat hesitantly wondering which slot, out of two, I should use. The patient seeing my predicament kindly helped me by motioning (pardon the pun) to the correct orifice under the boarded bed. Blushing furiously I thanked him, did the necessary, and left, wondering if that glint in his eye told me why he had chosen me?

As the day wore on I became aware that not only did the other nurses know more than me, but also the patients. And when I thought of the cleaners and the people who did voluntary work I felt very helpless! Of course your seniors are there to help you ... Aren't they?

And why, I asked myself had I been placed on a male ward? Surely I would have been safer to practice with my own sex? At least I would feel at home with their anatomical and mental needs.

Safely back in the Nurses Home at the end of the shift, found you exhausted, probably lying on a bed with one of your set (fresh out of training school like yourself) discussing how the day went.

The next day would find you on the same merry-go-round. This soon became as much a part of you as brushing your teeth, starting with the same routine jobs: toiletries for those unable to walk to the wash basins, bed making etc. But it was not boring, because each patient is an individual and by the time you had finished you had gained an insight into each patient's concerns or hopes. Bed making that you had practised so diligently in PTS now came to the fore. Yes, I could do hospital corners and knew which way to place the pillows. This was one area in which I felt hospitals would have liked to make the patient fit the bed, rather than vice versa. God help the patient who dared to move once their bed had been made!

We were, at that time, between the eras of choosing nursing as a vocation and nursing as an interesting field of science (but not total devotion for life). This seemed to be reflected in our pay, which for the time was not good. Room and meals were subtracted before you saw your pay packet. Any days off, mostly spent away from the hospital, were not reimbursed. My memory tells me that the sum left after deductions was around £6 per month, rising to £10 per month on successfully completing your State Registration.

There was this sub-culture running within the hospital, which at first passed me by. But as I progressed it was made pretty clear that to the previously trained, well-established nursing fraternity I was entering into a vocation. Boyfriends were to be discouraged at all costs.

We had to live-in, there was no option; we had to be in our rooms by 10pm. If not we would find ourselves outside Matron's office the next morning waiting to receive a third degree as to where we had been, and with whom. "And Nurse", Matron would say, "Do you really think that you are capable of looking after your patients properly if you've not had sufficient sleep?" Of course, times were changing, but the old brigade was not going out silently. If you wished to marry there was no way that you would be allowed to continue your training.

Things like: "Nurse, I've been a little worried; recently you don't seem to have your mind on the job". This was not done as a criticism but intoned to show concern. Various such innuendoes implying lack of total commitment were broached from time to time.

The door to the Nurses Home at the Norfolk and Norwich Hospital was locked at 10pm, sharp. The key was kept in Night-Sister's Office. Anyone arriving back late would therefore be required to request to be let in, thus bringing this indiscretion to the attention of the powers that be. But sometimes luck intervened. A passing nurse or junior doctor could sometimes be persuaded to find the key whilst Sister was on her rounds of the wards, and let you in. Or, and this was more perilous, you could wait until Sister left her office in the hospital, run up the corridor at the speed of sound, unlock the door, return the key, and run the length of the corridor again in the hope of not being caught. But the regime then, although authoritarian, allowed us enough freedom not to feel totally stifled, although it would not bode well with human rights and such-like these days.

We had to learn each wards' procedure as each had different needs according to the medical conditions treated there. How the men, on my first ward, lying on their flat wooden beds, outside on the balcony in all weathers, coped so cheerfully, I'll never know. They were bathed, all toiletries attended to, and took their meals all in the same horizontal position. Their endurance was to be applauded. These were our recovering tuberculosis patients. Now of course that harsh regime has been superseded by a course of tablets.

There was more of a family feel to this ward, mainly I think due to the long-stay patients. This consisted, apart from the TB patients, of the RTAs, (Road Traffic Accidents). They spent a lot more time on bed rest than now, and were also more inclined as they improved, to get bored and think up practical jokes as a way of passing the time.

My three months on Orthopaedics passed quickly and happily. I learned a lot in that time. Observation holds a vital role in nursing and maybe this has been somewhat over-shadowed these days by 'facts'. I think sometimes nurses actually forget that one important question: "How do you feel?" So often I hear people say that they know that there is something wrong, but because all the blood tests, x-rays, scans, and so on have come back normal the consultant tries to assure them that all is well.

When Matron, or Night Sister did their ward rounds we were expected to know down to the last detail, everything about each patient: diagnosis, treatment, marital status, and so on. It was surprising we were not asked where they did their weekly shop. But the thing is, we knew! Any relative checking on a patient would get an immediate update from one who knew. How often do you now hear these words: "Oh sorry, she's not one of mine. I'll try to find someone who knows". And do they?

My next ward placement was on Female Surgical, a far cry from my beloved Orthopaedics. The ward appeared a lot tidier, which I put down to the absence of pulleys and weights adorning every other bed. Neither was there the *bonhomie* between the patients, born of familiarity. I was surprised at how long it took me to adjust. But from there I went from ward to ward, from day duty to night duty, from hospital to hospital learning all the time. We were affiliated to the West Norwich and Jenny Lind and could find ourselves in transit, complete with suitcase when we were appointed to either of the other hospitals for a period of training.

Throughout our three-year training, lectures were set on an almost weekly basis, given, and exams marked, by our Consultants. If these fell on our precious days off, that was just tough. At times they would inevitably fall when we were on night duty. This would find us reluctantly hauling ourselves, bleary-eyed, down to the lecture hall. It was a case of attend or be damned, as receiving our hospital badge depended on these internal exam results; although we grumbled, we had no option. Times would change rapidly within the next ten years, indeed during my training. Of course most of us went on to achieve our ambition; fully qualified before marriage and then able to return as a working wife and mother, thanks to the realisation that this was the twentieth century and things must change.

Looking back I find it difficult to imagine how we accepted our fate without more complaints. We didn't think that all the rules mwere reasonable, but seemed to accept the conditions at that time. I'm sure there was nothing in our contracts agreeing to such draconian measures.

There were things I questioned and things I could see good reason for. But despite all this, the patients came first. Although rules were made that sometimes I felt did not enhance the well-being of the patient as a whole, nevertheless that was, at all times, the intention.

No one could foresee the momentous changes that would take place within the NHS. The advancement of such things as heart surgery followed by the tremendous cost that it entailed. Plastic being put to use in so many fields. Keyhole surgery allowing the patient to recover more quickly with less damage to their body. Antibiotics, which were used and at times overused. Neither could anyone have envisaged the demands to be made, beginning on that unforgettable day on July 5th in 1948, when the NHS was born.

The tempo in nursing was slow by today's standards. We were treating disease which was much more developed than it is today and therefore required more bed rest. The idea behind it was that once we had caught up with all these illnesses people were harbouring, often through poverty and lack of knowledge, the demands on the Health Service would lessen. Whoever said that?

Today it is so different: day operations have superseded for the majority and nursing care has changed out of necessity. It must be far more exhausting to greet new patients on a daily basis, without the chance to get to know them as individuals.

But the total number of people making their copious demands on the Health Service has increased beyond imagination. Therefore one of the aims now is to increase the number of patients treated (meeting your targets) in order to reduce waiting lists and improve health. Whilst this is commendable it nevertheless brings a sense of 'factory' to the hospitals. All these changes are of necessity not better, not worse, but different.

A Snapshot of Unthank Road in the 1940s

John Riseborough, born 1937

I was born at number 296, Dereham Road, Norwich; probably during a terrible thunderstorm because that's the way things go for me.

By the time I was two weeks old I was fighting for my life against double pneumonia and pleurisy. The blame for that was laid at the door of the district nurse who, it is alleged, bathed me in front of an empty grate in very cold weather. We won't dwell on that because she isn't here to defend herself. I have been told that I was so ill that my heart stopped beating, but luckily the doctor was there and he managed to re-start it. That was before the introduction of defibrillators and heart massage. I can only thank the doctor for being there at the right moment.

This all occurred in the days before the NHS and I wonder just how much it cost to keep me alive; probably a couple of steaks and a string of sausages because my Dad was a butcher and had his shop just into Merton Road, where there is now a hairdressers shop. Before I was born he had his first shop in Taverham, in the garden of a bungalow called 'West End' trading from a wooden garage. The bungalow is still there but I doubt if the wooden shop still exists.

Before I was born my parents had 3 children: two girls and a boy. Cynthia (Cinnie) was the eldest, born April 27th 1929 and was 8yrs old when I joined the family. Margaret, (Margie) was born on Nov 20th 1930 and Richard (Dick) was born June 12th 1932 (deceased 2004). They all attended the Wensum View School on Waterworks Road, but by the time I was old enough to go to school the family had moved to a new shop at 117, Unthank Road where my sister Carolyn was born on Christmas Eve 1938.

There were two more children later: Anne, (who had a twin brother, stillborn) was born at the Stork Nursing Home on Yarmouth Road, Thorpe, on Jan 24th 1944 and Thomas, always called Tom (deceased 2005) was the last, born in March 1946.

Number 117 Unthank Road is a tall house of 4 stories but it was still crowded with all of us. At the beginning of our residence there Dick was allocated the attic for his bedroom. Cinnie and Margie had the back bedroom and I suppose I was in a cot in the box room above the hallway, but I don't remember anything about that until Dick was relegated to a double bed with me in the box room, and a sort of passageway to the attic stairs was demolished to make the back bedroom larger. I can just remember that this passageway, leading to the attic stairs, was always full of evil-smelling shoes, had hooks for coats and some little square window panes high up to let in some light.

In the attic (after Dick moved out) was kept a lot of miscellaneous junk including an egg incubator from the days when dad kept 1000 chickens. This had been brought from Granddad Riseborough's house after it was bombed in 1942, along with a lot of other rubbish. Our gas masks were also stored there after the war and I particularly remember the one for Anne with a little pump on the side, because the whole child had to be enclosed in the gas mask and laced in.

The attic window was very small and it had 2 iron bars across to prevent anyone from falling out, but they were mighty rusty and I don't think they would have taken much of a strain. And it was a heck of a long way down to the ground (4 stories).

Next-door at 113 lived Mr & Mrs Reginald (Corkie) Bone with their son Peter. Mr. Bone worked at Todhouse Raynard in Redwell

Street, Norwich, next door to the City Arms pub. Todhouse Raynard was a high class tailor's shop and Corkie was very proud to have once made a Norfolk Jacket for somebody in the Royal family. In fact he never stopped bragging about going to measure whoever it was. They also specialised in making Officers' Dress Uniforms as well as the normal kit. During the war he used to do "Fire Watching" with Dad but I don't believe they did much watching: there were too many empty bottles about in the morning. They all played 'Newmarket' most of the night.

My childhood territory ranged from The Elms, at Park Lane on Unthank Road to Glebe Road and from Newmarket Street across to Avenue Road. Anywhere outside that rectangle was "Foreign Territory" where other gangs of kids weren't always friendly.

On the corner of Park Lane was the Park Tavern (now called the Lily Langtry) a Bullard's House. The brewer's dray that delivered their beer when I was an infant was a steam driven lorry with an enormous chain drive underneath. Next to the pub was Bilham's the newsagents who also sold stationery. They sometimes used to have little pads made from printer's off-cuts that we loved for 'jotters'. They also stocked pens, nibs, ink, pencils and rubbers and I'm sure I bought my first fountain pen there with some birthday money. It was a Golden Platignum, and boy, didn't I think I was somebody with that? This was all in the days before Biros and ballpoint pens and fibre-tips. I can remember the first Biro Pen I ever saw: it was in 1948 and a friend was given one when he passed the scholarship (11Plus). Most kids got a new bike, but a Biro was much more 'up market'. They cost over £20!

After Bilham's shop was Adcock's Electrical and Cycles where we used to take the radio accumulator to be charged up. They were connected by an inside door to Weaver's the Ironmongers next door. Mr Weaver was Mr Adcock's father-in-law and he kept bees in his back garden. He had a little puffer machine that made magic smoke (so he assured me) to send his bees to sleep so he could take all the honey without them knowing and without him being stung. But if I got too close I would get stung. I never got too close.

Next to Weaver's was an alleyway leading to Marjoram's yard. Marjoram's were carpenters and joiners and in later years joined up with Anderson's the builders who had a yard just round the corner in Park Lane.

The other side of the alley was Canham & Maine, the ladies fashion shop. They also sold some children's clothing and I remember having a struggle with my mum about a jumper that she wanted to buy for me. The name on the label was Jaeger, which I was told, is a German name. Well I wasn't going about in a German jumper when they keep dropping bombs on us and frightening everybody to death. I had to wear it though!

Next to this shop were a couple of private houses occupied by Mick McKenzie's family, and the Sinclairs who were related to them. Mick McKenzie was our assistant Scout Master in the 2nd Norwich Scout Troop. He was a terrific storyteller and a splendid teacher of the art and craft of 'back-woodsmanship'. He taught us a lot at scouts, like whipping the ends of ropes, knotting and splicing ropes, and lashing. He even made us tie knots behind our backs, so we would be able to do it in the dark, and then he suggested we do a back-splice behind our backs. That was very hard, but we eventually managed to do it.

Mick served throughout the war in the Artillery and reached the rank of Captain, serving in North Africa and was then involved in the Battle of Casino in Italy, where there were appalling losses capturing the Monastery on top of the mountain. Mick could tell wonderful yarns about his adventures in the desert. Somehow I got the impression he was a member of 'Popskies Private Army', a renowned behind the lines fighting force that became 'The Long Range Desert Group' causing many headaches for the enemy.

The next building was Mr Whitears shop. He was a butcher whose son Bobby was about Dick's age. Bobby had something that every boy envied - a full set of electric trains with all the ancillary equipment permanently set up in a shed in the garden. I was only allowed in to see it once but I believe I turned green with envy immediately.

Mr Whitear used to close his shop on Thursday afternoons, as did most shopkeepers in Norwich, and it was fun to run up to his door, ring the bell, and run like hell. But one day when it was my turn to press the bell button he was waiting. No sooner had I reached up to press the bell-push than the door opened and a hand came out and grabbed me. He hauled me inside and stung the back of my thigh where my short trousers ended, and then let me out. I tore home bawling and told my dad "Mr Whitear hit me!" Then my dad gave me another hiding for telling tales. That's what they call rough justice.

After Whitears the ground level dropped a bit to the "posh" shop of Bernard Brown, the gentlemen's outfitters. There were suits and shirts in the window, but I expect the most he sold were socks and hankies.

Joining Browns was Mason and Sabberton's, the hairdressers. Mr Mason was away fighting in the war, so his ground floor barber shop was closed until 1945 when he returned. But the ladies' hairdressers shop downstairs stayed open. Mr Mason was a very tall man who had to stoop when he cut men's hair, so it is hardly surprising that he didn't like cutting kid's hair, making him stoop even further. If a child was waiting for a haircut and a man came in the child was made to wait until the man was done. He had a little cupboard next to his mirror that contained objects called "Something for the weekend sir?" I was dying to see what they were!

When Mr Mason was away we sometimes went to another barber in Rupert Street and there is an amusing story about a family of boys having haircuts there. There were three of them and they went in for a haircut. The youngest was done first and when the barber asked for 1/- he said "My brother has the money". So the next brother was done and, in response to the request for 2/-, he said the same as the first: "My brother has the money". Finally the eldest got in the chair and had his short back and sides and then he gave the barber 1/-. That was 2/- short. They had spent the rest on sweets and eaten them all. Well the barber couldn't put the hair back on again so they were warned never to go there again. I often wonder how many times they pulled that trick with different barbers.

Mr Blackman our newsagent had the next shop. He had two boys, one of whom was called Brian who I sometimes played with. Mr Blackman had been in the army I think, but he must have come out before the end, probably wounded.

Now we come to the shop of old Mr Lovick. He was a shoe repairer and we spent many a happy hour watching him "eat the nails" and then spit them out again. I thought he resembled Geppetto in the Pinnochio story and he certainly liked having children about. I'm sure that if his door opened and he couldn't see the potential customer over his counter when he was sitting at his last, he knew it was either me or my sister Carolyn come to watch him repairing somebody's shoes.

Next door to him was a grocer shop-cum-dairy. The most vivid memory I have of this shop is the square tins along the front of the counter with their glass-topped lids; you could see all the goodies they contained, and sometimes they would sell, for a penny, the broken ones. In this shop they sold milk, cheese and bacon and it was fascinating to watch them pat a blob of butter into a cube ready to be wrapped in greaseproof paper. This shop changed hands when I was little and was next owned by a Mr & Mrs Woor who had a son of about my age, called Eddie.

Behind all these shops were some lock-up garages with access via Rose Valley. Most of these lock-ups were in use as storage for the shops and one day Eddie and I found some sand and cement to play with. So we mixed it up and filled all the keyholes with the mixture, not realising what would happen when it dried. I believe somebody from Barnard's Engineering Works had seen us and reported it when it became apparent what had happened. Anyway, a policeman came to see me: need I say more?

The dairy had a sweet shop next door and this also changed hands at about the same time. It was taken over by Mr Woor's brother. He had a hatch made especially for the sale of ice-creams and above the hatch was an enormous cornet as an advert. I always wanted to say: "I'll have one like that," and point up to it, but I was too shy.

These four shops were all in a block with a passageway at each end for access to the rear of the houses. The next building belonged to the Norwich Co-operative Society, and they had two shops. These were a Butcher's Shop and a Grocery Department. I don't think I ever went into the Butcher's; I suppose it was a kind of family loyalty. But I did frequent the Grocery Department next door. They weighed up sugar into little blue bags and sold Brooke Bond Tea in little brown packets tied up with string. There was always a chair for the harassed housewife to sit on while her order was being made up, and everything was weighed or counted while you waited. The customer was always asked what her "Divi" number was, but I never knew we had one or what "Divi" meant.

Out on the edge of the pavement, near the Co-op, stood a policeman's call box. This was a tall blue cast-iron pillar with a triangular top that held a telephone, from where a policeman could call in to HQ for instructions or advice; on one of the other sides was an emergency call-box for the general public. You just had to pull open the door and a voice would say: "Which service do you require?" That was a good game if we could reach by standing on somebody's back.

Next came Rose Valley. The pub named after it was on the corner opposite the Co-op. On the right going down the hill is a large open area with the lock-ups already mentioned, and Barnard's Engineering works was at the rear of the open area. They did a lot of work for the Royal Navy, making propeller screws among other things. I never could understand how they made props on a lathe, but I saw it with my own eyes. There were always heaps of coils of steel swarfe outside going rusty, and if you played with it you would get a nasty cut because it was very sharp. It was fascinating to watch the lathes working and the men pouring some sort of milky, oily fluid onto the cutter when it started smoking. They used to ask me if I wanted a drink of the milk!

For such a small area Rose Valley had an amazing number of inhabitants: all the little houses must have been two up and two down with shared outside toilets. There was a tiny shop belonging to Mrs Neal. Her shop was a lifesaver for our family because if ever Mum ran out of anything in the way of groceries, it was usually on a Sunday morning when all the other shops were closed. But if you banged loud enough on Mrs Neal's door she would open up and sell you a tin of Burdall's or a loaf of bread or some candles. You name it and she had some somewhere in her shop! She stocked coal in little sacks. The bread she sold was always a bit burnt on top, but it was delicious.

When VE day came we were allowed to have a bonfire and let off fireworks. One boy decided that the bonfire would be built on top of a man-hole cover in the widest part of the 'Valley', so we little kids scoured the district for anything that would burn and dragged it to him for building up. The final heap was enormous, made up from any old wood we found and old mattresses and clothes. I reckon some of the clothes we burned were better than those we were wearing. The crowning glory of this wonderful conflagration was a stuffed dummy dressed up to look like Adolph Hitler. The bonfire was duly lit at dusk and the little demons, golden rain, roman candles and rockets went up in smoke in double quick time. As far as I can recall only one casualty occurred. Somebody put a squib into the coat-belt of a boy from Park Lane, and it burnt a hole in his coat. We put some spuds into the embers to roast but unfortunately it was bedtime before they were done so somebody else got the benefit of them. The manhole cover was a bit bent when all the ash was cleared away and it rattled when a bike rode over it. So the authorities replaced it just in time for VJ night when we did the bonfire bit all over again!

There was an air raid shelter on the corner in the 'Valley', surrounded by iron railings. Those railings weren't taken away for munitions like most of the garden railings round about and one day a boy fell on them while trying to get off the roof of the shelter. One of the spikes went right into his thigh and he had to be lifted off by an adult and taken to hospital. I don't think any lasting damage was done, but I still feel all juddery when I think about it, and he had an enormous scar.

Between the shelter and Barnard's was a row of little cottages with a narrow access passageway. Mr Doughty lived in one of theses houses: a chubby little man who sometimes did a meat round for Dad, making deliveries on our trade bike. He was also a porter at the Norfolk and Norwich Hospital. His party trick was to run with the trade bike until he had a bit of momentum and then leap into the saddle without touching the pedals. If he hadn't got it just right it would have been very painful.

Coming back onto Unthank Road the Rose Valley pub was on the right. This was a Lacon's House run by Mr and Mrs Towlson. There was an Air Raid Shelter in the garden of the pub, down some steps from Unthank Road.

The last house in Primrose Place belonged to the Adcock family. There were two boys; the eldest was Ivan and he was most noteworthy for the little miniature barrage balloon system he rigged up in their garden, hanging them from the trees. These little balloons were made of the real material but were stuffed to shape with cotton wool and were hung on cotton threads. It was, if you had any imagination, lifelike.

There was another shoe repair shop. This was where you took your shoes if you wanted your new soles stitched on, rather than nailed by Mr Lovick. They charged a little more too, because they employed another man who could work the sewing machine.

A little haberdashery came next and I think it was a Miss Neal. She sold all sorts of wool and cloth material, cottons, buttons, pins and needles, knitting and dressmaking patterns and lots of other things ladies liked to buy.

Beside this shop was a wide driveway to Mrs Scott's house that was set back from the row of houses on Unthank Road. There was a huge gate, such as you would find in a field, and in the garden was a big pear tree with a rope swing. Mrs Scott had some Dutch refugee children staying with her at one stage of the war and I couldn't understand why they weren't wearing clogs if they were really Dutch. They did talk in a rather strange tongue that none of us could fathom out, but perhaps they weren't German spies after all. I liked playing in her garden because it was very child friendly.

I believe the hairdressers shop the other side of Scotty's drive was called Rita's. I never had occasion to go in there and I would never have voluntarily gone in, judging by the awful pong that came out when the door was opened. According to a notice on the window they claimed to do "Marcel Waving". If you put your nose right on the window glass you would be able to see those huge hairdryers, like beehives, that ladies liked getting their heads into.

Next to Rita's came Matthes the bakers shop. Their window was always full of scrumptious-looking cakes. I always enjoyed what I think were called Savoy Buns, as well as Chelsea Buns and Eccles cakes. The doughnuts were out of this world and were very rare. If there were any available I had my share of them too. I can't remember any of the cakes being rationed during the war.

Next was the closed down shop of Mr Punchard, the fish and chip merchant. It was closed down because he too was away serving in the forces against Hitler's best. When the blitz was at its height the authorities erected a huge steel reservoir in front of his shop for an emergency water supply for fire-fighting in case the mains were ruptured. There was a wire netting cover over the top to stop me falling in and the panels of steel were sealed watertight with a kind of black mastic which, if it got on your hands then it got everywhere. And I mean *everywhere*! The only thing able to remove it was butter - and whose Mum would give him some precious butter to put on *himself*?

My best pal Georgie Yallop's Dad had the next shop. He was a fruit and vegetable merchant of the old school. His spuds still had the dirt on them! We had a lot of wonderful adventures in their back garden amid the round Covent Garden 'coster's' baskets and the disused chicken houses, climbing over great mountains of sacks of spuds. The next door garden of Burrell's the builders was a wonderful playground too, because Mr Burrell was also away fighting. We spent countless happy hours there, being just about anybody from Robin Hood to Dick Turpin or Robinson Crusoe. The only drawback in Burrell's garden was the stinging nettles. These were enormous, way above my head, waving about in the breeze. One day, when we were standing on the embankment at the top of the garden, looking down on these nettles, Georgie dared me to jump into them and, fool that I am, I jumped. It was summertime and I was only wearing a vest and short trousers with sandals, no socks. I was stung from head to toe, and there weren't enough dock leaves in the world to take away the pain! I ran home, bawling, but there was nothing anybody could do, I just had to put up with it.

There used to be an outhouse at the back of Burrell's shop. Well Georgie and I pretended we were demolition men and with a couple of lumps of wood we demolished this outhouse completely. There was nothing left except the water tap standing on its lead pipe alone. I suppose they put it down to bomb damage when Mr Burrell came home, and the insurance would have paid out. Anyway, the policeman never came to see me about that one!

Miss Smith had her newsagent's shop next to Burrell's. Hers was a very dark shop inside and there were three counters. From the one on the left she dispensed newspapers, magazines and comics and from the one on the right the cigarettes and pipe tobacco were sold. I used to have to go there to buy Dad's 'Players Please' - 100 at a time if she had them and 50 if she didn't. The counter opposite the door was for pencils, pens, nibs, ink and stationery. I did a newspaper round for her when I was older.

Miss Smith was also something big in the Red Cross. I remember her coming to help when Mum got herself hung up on a meat hook in our shop by accident. Apparently Mum was reaching up to re-hang another bit of meat when she lost her balance and her hand caught on an empty hook next to the one she had just put up. I think the hook went into her wrist just where you feel for the pulse, so it didn't half bleed!

My sister Margie joined the Red Cross too, intending to go into nursing when she left school, but her first job was at Larkman Nursery School, and then she went right off nursing and became a shorthand typist after a course at Underwood's School. Her first aid training came in handy when I cut my finger on one of Dad's knives when I'd been sharpening a pencil.

The Home & Colonial was the next emporium; I always thought of it as a 'posh Co-op'. There was always a wonderful aroma in a real grocers shop: bacon, cheese, butter and dried peas all mixed together. They would cut you a piece of cheese with a wire, and slice your bacon on a machine that whizzed round at lightening speed and could take off your hand if you got the rhythm wrong.

The final shop in this long row belonged to Mr Hurn the chemist. Or rather, it was one of Mr Hurn's shops because he also had one in Rupert Street on the corner with Trinity Street. He was a special friend of Dad's because they were in the same Home Guard Unit.

After Hurn's chemist shop there was a row of private terraced houses, the first of which was a little private school called Cambridge House, owned and run by Mr Mac Farlane.

A little further along, on the corner of Portland Street was another butcher's shop called Chapman's. Mr Chapman was quite old when we were little and when he retired my Dad bought the business and transferred it to our shop. Among all the equipment that came with it was his Austin 7 van which Dad called "Puddlejumper". I had my first driving lessons in that van and the first and second gears weren't syncro-mesh. It took quite a bit of practice to get it just right with the "double de-clutching" when changing gear.

On the corner of Trinity Street and opposite the Park Tavern (Lily Langtree) was a garage with petrol pumps and opposite that was Dr Taylor's surgery. He was our doctor and used to prescribe a kind of lemon-coloured sweet water for nearly every illness. I suffered a lot from sties on my eyelids and I half expected him to tell me to rub in some of this magic potion. But it never actually came to that because the golden eye ointment from the chemist's always worked.

On the corner of Gloucester Street was the shop of Lilian Smith, the Ladies' Fashion Shop. I never went in the shop but on a Sunday afternoon after Sunday School sometimes Mrs Smith would let about a dozen of us little kids go up into her attic where her son would show some old silent films on his little 8mm projector. We had to pay 1d or 2d because he hired the films from somewhere in Norwich. There were Laurel & Hardy, Charlie Chaplin, Buster Keaton and such like. We thought it was wonderful and looked forward to the next time as soon as one show finished. Then when the film show ended we descended from the attic and Mrs Smith would make her cuckoo clock perform for us. He cucked and -ooed all the way round the clock face much to our delight, and, occasionally, was persuaded to do it all over again.

On the other side of Gloucester Street was the Post Office and then on the corners of Onley Street and Unthank Road was Sewell's a bakers shop, and across the road Waller's, another grocer's shop. Waller's were the first people in our area to stock "Birds Eye Fro Fruits" which were iced lollies without a stick. They were just wrapped in silver foil and were scrumptious.

The final shop along Unthank Road was another chemist's shop on the corner of Bury Street. I can remember getting Horlick's Tablets, Ovaltine Tablets and Zubes there when my sweet coupons ran out and all the other shops had sold out. I would also settle for Ex-Lax Chocolate if they had nothing else, but it never had the expected effect on me. On the corner of Mount Pleasant was a pub called Eaton Cottage, and then even further along, just opposite Glebe Road was Emms' Garage where we sometimes took our bikes to have punctures mended.

Just before D-Day we had all sorts of servicemen billeted in the big houses opposite the long row of shops. Some were British Tommies with their little Bren-Gun Carriers and some were American soldiers. We used to follow the Yanks chanting "Got any gum Chum?" and it usually worked; we'd get a packet of Wrigley's to share between us.

There were also some British servicemen in Blue Uniform Suits who had been wounded. This was the official hospital uniform, so people wouldn't ask awkward questions about why they were at home and not in the fighting.

Before the war really got into gear we were able to buy ice creams. I believe we could get them from Matthes bakers shop along the road and they were made by J.J. Lyons. They were little rolls of ice cream wrapped in paper. The paper was taken off and the ice cream popped into a cornet. One day I was enjoying my penny cornet when a wasp decided he wanted to share it, which I wasn't prepared to do. So he stung me on the eyeball and then he got *all* the ice cream.

When Carolyn and I were old enough we had to attend Sunday School at the Parochial Hall in Gloucester Street on Sunday afternoons. Then, when we got home we were each given 3d to "go for a bus ride". We would have to get on the bus outside Matthes bakers shop on Unthank Road, pay a 1½d fare and ride through the city to Wall Road where we would get off, get on again, pay another 1½ d and ride home. But we got it wrong! We were too quick. "Why didn't you go for a walk when you got there?" Because nobody said anything about going for a walk, and anyway how were we supposed to know mother and father wanted 'time to themselves'?

91

On the return journey from Wall Road the bus always made a long stop outside Purdy's the bakers on Gentleman's Walk, for the driver and conductor to change over. Above Purdy's door was a wooden carving of three chefs with wooden spoons which always fascinated me. Also at the Haymarket was a statue of Thomas Browne the famous Norwich philosopher and doctor of medicine sitting in his armchair.

While Sunday school is in focus, I was in the church choir for a brief period. My brother Dick was head choirboy and I was roped in as soon as I was old enough. He got £1 a month and the most I ever got was 2/6 a month, because I preferred playing soldiers on the bomb sites to singing at choir practice on a Friday night, and practices counted in the wage as well as Sunday services.

Before I started proper school I was never at home because I had discovered some good friends in Mrs Boswell, who lived opposite the shop at number 120, on the corner of York Street, and Mrs Towlson whose husband was the landlord of the Rose Valley pub. It seemed to me that Mr Boswell never went to work. He was always up in his little attic workshop building radio sets. I was too young to know about retirement and he had been in the merchant navy as an engineer and now just did some occasional marine insurance work. I will always remember the smell of hot soldering irons and soldering flux. I spent many hours just watching him working and I now remember how he used to build little television sets. He 'acquired' a wooden cabinet and made a TV set for us when we moved to College Road in the 1950s, just after the Coronation. He also had a nice shed in the garden with a proper lathe.

Mr Boswell built a caravan in the backyard. I helped, by holding, when I was told to hold, and letting go when I was told to let go! That caravan was built beneath two enormous beech trees and I'm afraid I spent a lot of time searching through the beech-nut husks looking for nuts. I'd like to think that the caravan would have been built quicker if I'd been more attentive, but I really don't think I made much difference.

My other "special" friend was Mrs Towlson who lived at the Rose Valley pub and I spent many happy hours there. She had two sons who were in the armed forces. Arthur was the eldest and was named after his Dad, but was always called "Sonny". He was in the Fleet Air Arm, flying those old string bags called Swordfish, and, later Barracudas, off aircraft Carriers. Arthur was awarded the DSO for his part in the sinking of the Tirpitz. I can remember him bringing a crewmate home on leave with him once who, I'm pretty sure, came from New Zealand. Later in the war this friend may have been killed or injured because Sonny once brought home a flying boot that had a hole in it and a lot of blood in the sheep's wool lining: a pretty gruesome keepsake. He showed me where there was a little pocket in the lining that held a tiny knife. Those boots were designed so that if an airman was brought down he could use the knife to cut off the top of the boots and convert them into a pair of shoes.

Sonny has told me that he twice had to land his 'plane in the sea. Once because of engine failure and the second time was when he was given wrong information about the wind direction and strength that completely upset his navigation. He couldn't make it back to the carrier so was forced to ditch in the sea. But at least he survived to tell the tale!

The other son, Geoffrey was in the RAF. He was a Sergeant pilot, later promoted to Warrant Officer. One day when I was in their house we had to rush outside when a lot of 'planes flew over and one of them 'waggled' its wings. Mrs Towlson said that was Geoff; he had told her he was going to fly over, but he would have been in trouble if anybody knew this. At the later stages of the war Geoff was flying an American twin-engine bomber called a Mitchell in the 2nd Air Division during the Battle of the Bulge.

I spent a lot of time in the Rose Valley pub, either standing on a box washing glasses behind the bar, or downstairs playing with the super toys that were kept on a shelf high up in the pantry, still in their original boxes. There were lead soldiers in First World War uniforms, with field guns that could fire matchsticks, and lorries with little trailers, some cowboys and Indians and a wonderful Hornby Train set.

When I had a couple of ha'pennies in my pocket I would just keep rattling them because I was too shy to ask if I could buy a bag of Smiths Crisps. They didn't always have any because there was a terrible shortage of crisps during the war, but when there were some they were kept in a glass jar on the shelf in the 'Bottle & Jug', which was a tiny servery between the bar and the lounge. I also loved a drink that Mrs Towlson sometimes made up for me. It was orange squash mixed with soda-water from a glass soda siphon.

Although I loved crisps, I also had a love affair with chips - potato chips, cooked properly, in beef dripping in a chip shop with lots of 'crispy bits' stuck to them and plenty of salt, no vinegar please! The nearest Fish & Chip shop was Punchard's, but his shop was closed for the duration. There was another, hardly a stone's throw away, in Gloucester Street on the corner of Trix Road. This was Cheeseman's and they opened every night except Thursdays. But that didn't matter because on Thursdays another shop a mere two hundred yards further up Gloucester Street, called Royals, was open.

During the winter of 1947 we had a lot of snow and it lasted for many weeks. I recall seeing men from the Labour Exchange coming along with shovels, cutting the packed snow on the pavements and loading it onto lorries to be taken elsewhere to melt. But they didn't take the snow from York Street, and it was a good thing too because we used to ride our sledges down York Street hill and across Unthank Road onto the plain in front of Robinson's shop. How it was that nobody went across the main road when a bus was coming, I don't know. We never gave it a thought, but that could have been a tragic accident waiting to happen. Sometimes a lady in the first house up the hill would scatter fire ashes across the pavement to melt the ice outside her gate, but we soon covered the ashes with more snow.

During this big freeze we had a terrible job getting fuel. There was a shortage of coal for some reason, so we had to scavenge for anything that would burn. Word would go round if Dodgers, near Potters Pickles Factory in Coach & Horses Street, had any coal and off we had to go with our sledge to get some, or anything else that would burn. Dodgers were general dealers and their shop was like an Aladdin's Cave. I recall above the door to the emporium was a wooden propeller from an old aeroplane. And inside the shop were a lot of old bikes, for rent if you had the money. They had some penny farthings in there, and Mr Dodger even made a bike out of an old brass bedstead once!